P9-EJZ-574

Eyewitness
PIRATE

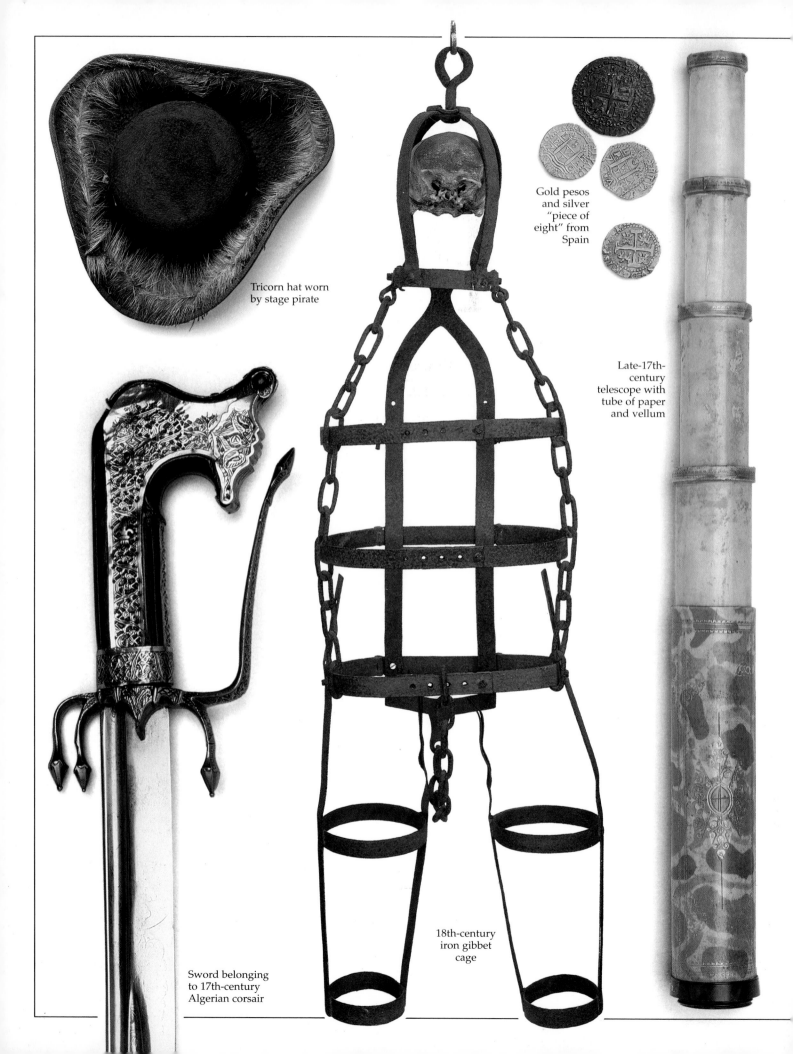

Tricorn hat worn by stage pirate

Gold pesos and silver "piece of eight" from Spain

Late-17th-century telescope with tube of paper and vellum

Sword belonging to 17th-century Algerian corsair

18th-century iron gibbet cage

Ring with skull-
and-crossbones
motif

Eyewitness
PIRATE

Gold
rings taken as
pirates' booty

Written by
RICHARD PLATT

Photographed by
TINA CHAMBERS

Sloop, the
type of vessel
used by pirates
in the Caribbean

Powder flask
with the cross
of the Knights
of St. John

3 1336 09875 0228

DK
DK Publishing, Inc.

Mariner's compass
with ivory case

Cloak of a
17th-century
gentleman pirate

Pair of flintlock pistols

17th-century
buccaneer's
cutlass

DK

LONDON, NEW YORK, MUNICH,
MELBOURNE, and DELHI

Project editor Bridget Hopkinson
Art editor Ann Cannings
Managing editor Simon Adams
Managing art editor Julia Harris
Researcher Céline Carez
Production Catherine Semark
Picture research Giselle Harvey
Consultant David Cordingly

REVISED EDITION
Category publisher Andrea Pinnington
Managing editors Andrew Macintyre, Camilla Hallinan
Managing art editors Jane Thomas, Martin Wilson
Editors Francesca Baines, Sue Nicholson
Art editor Catherine Goldsmith
Production Jenny Jacoby, Georgina Hayworth
Picture research Angela Anderson, Kate Lockley
DTP designers Siu Yin Ho, Andy Hilliard
US editor Elizabeth Hester
Senior editor Beth Sutinis
Art director Dirk Kaufman
US production Chris Avgherinos
US DTP designer Milos Orlovic

This Eyewitness ® Guide has been conceived by
Dorling Kindersley Limited and Editions Gallimard

This edition published in the United States in 2007
by DK Publishing, 375 Hudson Street, New York, New York 10014

A catalog record for this book is available from
the Library of Congress.

ISBN 978-0-7566-3005-8 (HC) 978-0-7566-0712-8 (Library Binding)

Color reproduction by Colourscan, Singapore
Printed in China by Toppan Printing Co. (Shenzhen), Ltd.

Discover more at
www.dk.com

A navigator's
astronomical
compendium

A hoard of
pirate treasure

Contents

17th-century French treasure chest

Robbers of the seas

WHO WERE THE PIRATES? Daring figures who swooped on treasure ships and returned home with golden cargoes? Brutal sea thieves who showed no mercy to their victims? Bold adventurers who financed travel by nautical theft? In fact, they were all these and more. The term "pirate" means simply "one who plunders on the sea," but those who led this sort of life fell into several categories: "privateers" were sea raiders with a government license to pillage enemy ships; "buccaneers" were 17th-century pirates who menaced the Spanish in the Caribbean; "corsairs" were privateers and pirates who roved the Mediterranean. In the words of Bartholomew Roberts (p. 39), all were lured by the promise of "plenty..., pleasure..., liberty and power."

SWASHBUCKLING HERO
A few real pirates lived up to their traditional swashbuckling image. Bold and brilliant Welsh pirate Howell Davis used daring ruses to capture ships off Africa's Guinea coast in 1719.

A TEMPTING TARGET
The East Indiamen – big ships trading between Europe and Asia – provided some of the most tempting targets for pirates. In earlier times, the capture of a Spanish galleon carrying treasure from the Americas was many a pirate's sweetest dream.

Wealthy East India companies decorated the sterns of their merchantmen with gold

PIRATES OF THE SILVER SCREEN
Hollywood pirate films have often blurred the lines between fact and fiction. In *Blackbeard the Pirate*, Blackbeard is pursued by Henry Morgan, who looks surprisingly well for a man who had in fact been dead for 30 years!

PROMISE OF RICHES
This illustration from Robert Louis Stevenson's pirate story *Treasure Island* (p. 60) shows the heroes loading sacks full of pirate treasure. Although there were many myths surrounding piracy, the vast fortunes in gold and silver so often depicted were really captured by some pirates. Pirates could become millionaires overnight, but they usually spent their booty as soon as they acquired it.

Cannon is balanced on this circular pivot

Pushing in wedge aims cannon lower

A HARD LIFE

Sailors of the 17th and 18th centuries found life at sea hard and dangerous, and, like "Poor Jack" in this poem, many never made it home again. Seamen were often tricked or kidnapped by naval press gangs into serving on men-of-war, where they were subjected to appalling conditions and harsh discipline. Compared to this, a pirate's life offered freedom and easy money, and many pirate crews were made up of formerly honest seamen.

"Poor Jack" going away to sea, perhaps never to return

POOR JACK.

PIRATES OF THE IMAGINATION

Pirates have captured the imaginations of many writers and artists over the years. The American illustrator Howard Pyle (1853–1911) portrayed the pirates and buccaneers of the 17th century in colorful and authentic detail. This evocative picture epitomizes the traditional image of the flamboyant pirate captain.

A rope was attached to the end of the grappling iron

BARBAROUS BRUTES?

The definition of a "pirate" often depended on which country you belonged to. This painting shows evil-looking Barbary corsairs attacking a helpless English crew. To the Europeans, the Barbary corsairs were brutal heathen pirates, but in North Africa, they were seen as legal privateers.

RULE OF TERROR

Pirates had a reputation for cruelty that many of them lived up to. They knew that their victims would surrender more easily if resistance was punished by torture and death. The buccaneers in particular were notorious for their brutality.

DARING THE DEVIL

Popular pirate tales such as those found in Charles Elms's *The Pirate's Own Book* (p. 61) encouraged the "superstitious horror connected with the name of pirate." In this illustration from Elms's book, a reckless pirate captain offers the devil a handful of his hair in return for a fair wind.

DANGER SIGNAL

A cannon shot was the signal for a ship to show its colors or be treated as an enemy. Pirates often tricked their victims by running up the colors of a friendly nation.

18th-century cannon that belonged to French corsair René Duguay-Trouin (p. 50)

GRAPPLING FOR GOLD

Swung into the rigging on the end of a rope, a grappling iron helped pirates to draw their victims' ship close enough for boarding. But pirates only did this as a last resort, preferring to make victims surrender by a show of force.

Barbed points are designed to lodge securely in the rigging of another ship

Pirates of Ancient Greece

SOME OF THE WORLD'S GREAT CIVILIZATIONS grew up around the Mediterranean and Aegean seas. Unfortunately for peoples of the ancient world, these waters were home to marauding sea robbers. The Aegean, at the center of the Greek world, was ideal for pirates. They hid among its countless tiny islands and inlets and preyed on passing trade ships. Piracy was fairly easy for these early sea raiders because merchant vessels hugged the coast and never crossed the open ocean. If the pirates waited long enough on a busy trade route, a valuable prize would eventually sail past. Pirates also attacked villages, kidnapping people to ransom or sell as slaves. But as Greek city-states gained power, they built strong navies that tried to keep pirates under control.

PIRATE ATTACK
The painting on this Greek bowl shows early pirates in action. When it was painted 2,500 years ago, pirate attacks were common throughout the Aegean, and there was little distinction between piracy and warfare. Later, when Greek city-states tried to impose order, pirates disguised their raids as reprisals – the custom of retaliating against attacks without actually declaring war.

Lumbering merchant ship under full sail

Fast pirate galley powered by oars

Sharp ram of the pirate galley drives into the side of the merchant ship

Athenian drinking bowl, 6th century B.C.

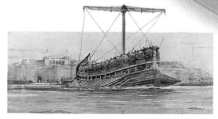

ASSYRIAN GALLEY
The Assyrians, who lived in what is now Iraq and Syria, probably attacked pirates in the Mediterranean in ships like this. However, no one knows for sure exactly what these vessels looked like.

THE PHOENICIANS FIGHT BACK
The Phoenicians carried out a thriving sea trade from the cities of Tyre and Sidon (in present-day Lebanon) in the 7th and 6th centuries B.C. Their merchant ships carried luxury cargoes such as silver, tin, copper, and amber to every corner of the Mediterranean. However, Greek pirates were a serious threat to Phoenician shipping, and war galleys, such as the one shown on this Phoenician coin, right, were used to defend trade interests.

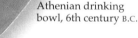

Silver shekels from the Phoenician city of Tyre

A HOARD OF SILVER
Ships from Phoenicia carrying luxury goods around the Mediterranean were obvious targets for early pirates. Lucky pirates might have captured a cargo of Spanish silver, which was used to make Phoenician coins like these.

A PIRATE VESSEL OF ANCIENT GREECE
This atmospheric photograph shows a replica of a Greek pirate galley. Pirates of the ancient world did not build special vessels, but relied on whatever was locally available. They used all kinds of ships, but preferred light, shallow-bottomed galleys that were fast and easy to maneuver. If pirates were pursued, their shallow boats enabled them to sail over rocks near the shore, where larger vessels could not follow.

PIRATES IN MYTHOLOGY
A Greek myth tells of a band of foolish pirates who captured Dionysus, the god of wine, hoping to ransom him. But the god took on the shape of a lion, and the terrified pirates threw themselves into the sea. As a punishment, Dionysus turned the pirates into a school of frolicking dolphins, pictured in this mosaic. The same story appears in Roman mythology, but the god is called Bacchus.

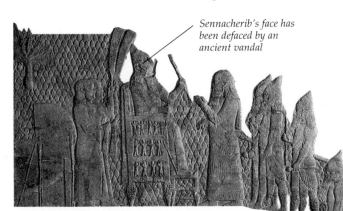

Sennacherib's face has been defaced by an ancient vandal

SENNACHERIB, SCOURGE OF PIRATES
In 694 B.C., the Assyrian king Sennacherib (ruled 704–681 B.C.), above, waged war against Chaldean sea raiders who had taken refuge in his kingdom on the coast of Elam, at the northern end of the Persian Gulf. His campaign successfully ended this seaborne threat.

ALEXANDER THE GREAT
Pirates roamed the Aegean when Alexander the Great (356–323 B.C.), right, ruled over Greece. In 331 B.C., he ordered them to be cleared from the seas. The great warrior king reputedly asked a captured pirate what reason he had for making the seas unsafe. The pirate replied, "The same reason as you have for troubling the whole world. But since I do it in a small ship, I am called a pirate. Because you do it with a great fleet, you are called an emperor."

MEDITERRANEAN MERCHANT SHIP
Ancient Greek trading vessels were no match for the sleek, streamlined galleys of the pirates who harassed them. Powered by square sails, merchant ships were easily overtaken by fast oar-driven pirate craft.

Terracotta model of a merchant ship, 6th century B.C.

Hull is broad and rounded to provide maximum cargo space

Pirates of the Roman world

"SAIL IN AND UNLOAD, your cargo is already sold!" With this slogan the Aegean port of Delos lured merchant ships – and pirates. The bustling port was part of the great Roman Empire, which flourished between about 200 B.C. and A.D. 476. In the Delos market, pirates sold kidnapped slaves and stolen cargoes to wealthy Romans who asked no questions. However, in the 1st century B.C., pirates posed a growing menace to trading vessels in the Mediterranean. When piracy threatened imports of grain to Rome, the people demanded action. In 67 B.C., a huge fleet of ships led by Pompey the Great (106 B.C.–48 B.C.) rounded up the sea pirates, while the Roman army stormed their base in Cilicia. This campaign solved Rome's immediate problems, but pirates remained a menace.

Deck rail

Oarsmen in the Roman navy were free men, not slaves

Lower deck was hot and smelly

Cutaway of a trireme

THE TRIREME
The warships that Rome sent against the pirates closely resembled Greek galleys. They were probably sleek triremes powered by three banks of oarsmen. Armed with a sharp ramming prow, these light vessels were fast and easy to handle in the calm waters of the Mediterranean. Trireme means literally "three-oar," probably because of the three-tier system of rowers.

KIDNAPPED
In about 75 B.C. the young Julius Caesar (c.102–44 B.C.) was captured by pirates while traveling to Rhodes to study. The pirates held him captive on a tiny Greek island for more than five weeks until his ransom was paid. After his release, Caesar took his revenge by tracking down the pirates and crucifying them.

Silver denarius, an ancient Roman coin, bearing Caesar's portrait

Gaul
Spain
Illyricum
Africa

ROMAN WORLD
This map shows how the Roman empire at its height stretched around the entire Mediterranean.

Corbita's hold might contain luxuries on its return from Italy

SLOW BOAT
Rome's grain fleet was mostly made up of broad, rounded corbitae like this one. Mediterranean pirates would have had little trouble hijacking these slow, heavily laden vessels as they sailed around the coast from Alexandria and Carthage to Ostia, the port that served Rome.

PRIZE WHEAT
Pirates attacking a Roman grain ship might be rewarded with a cache of emmer, above, a variety of wheat grown in the ancient world. Such cargoes could be sold at a profit in local markets.

ROMAN RENEGADE
Son of the famed pirate hunter Pompey the Great, Sextus Pompeius (67–36 B.C.) turned pirate to combat his political rival Octavian. From his base in Sicily, he raided and blockaded the Italian coast with great success. He claimed the title Ruler of the Sea until he was defeated by Octavian.

Long oars propel the trireme through the water at great speed

Eye

THE EVIL EYE
Like the Greek sea raiders before them, pirates of the Roman world preferred swift, agile galleys. The galley in this Roman fresco has eyes painted on the prow for "seeing" its prey. The eye symbol may have originated in Egypt as a superstitious good-luck charm.

DESIGN CLASSIC
The Romans were not natural sailors like the Greeks, whose island existence forced them into a maritime life. Roman shipbuilders, therefore, introduced few changes to the basic design of the war galley, right. To design warships for the Roman navy's drive against the pirates, shipbuilders simply copied the best designs of vessels from the past.

The amphora shape allowed for many to be wedged firmly in the hold of a ship

Handle for lifting jar in and out of the hold

AMPHORAE GLORY
Mediterranean cargo ships provided pirates with a huge variety of booty. The Romans imported large quantities of valuable wine and olive oil that were transported in pottery jars called amphorae.

PERSIAN PIRATE HUNTER
While the Mediterranean was fairly safe for Roman shipping, the Persian Gulf was not. King Shapur II of Persia (309–379) waged a ruthless war on pirates in this area. He was reputedly nicknamed Zulaklaf, which means "Lord of the shoulders," because legend has it that he pierced the shoulders of captured pirates and roped them all together like beads on a necklace.

Viking arrowheads

Raiders of the North

THE SAIL OF A VIKING SHIP looming on the horizon struck terror into the people of 9th-century northern Europe. It warned that dangerous Viking pirates would soon land. These fearsome Scandinavian warriors preyed on shipping routes and raided villages far inland. Since ancient times, the coastal tribes of Scandinavia had lived by robbing merchant ships. So when they began crossing the open sea, it was natural for them to pillage foreign coasts. Thg Vikings roamed the North Sea from the late 8th century to the early 12th century in search of booty. They were not the first northern raiders, nor the last. As long as merchant ships carried valuable cargoes, pirates were never far behind.

BATTLE AX
The ax was the favorite weapon of the Vikings. In the hands of a seasoned warrior, the large broad-ax could fell a man with a single blow. For fighting at sea, Vikings preferred a medium-sized ax that was easier to handle when boarding another vessel.

Silver decoration indicates that this ax was a symbol of prestige and power

THE SAXON THREAT
Five centuries before the Vikings began to terrorize northern Europe, Saxon pirates from the Baltic Sea plagued coasts and shipping. The Saxon raiders forced England's Roman rulers to strengthen their fleets and fortify much of England's eastern coast. Saxon ships, like the one above, had flat bottoms so that they could be rowed up shallow rivers for surprise attacks.

THE BLACK MONK
Legends claim that the 13th-century pirate Eustace the Monk had formed a pact with the devil and could make his ship invisible. But his magical powers apparently were not strong enough. Leading an invading fleet against England, Eustace was caught and beheaded at sea.

Geometric patterns of inlaid copper and silver

SPEAR CATCHERS
A Viking trick that terrified opponents was to catch a spear in midflight and hurl it straight back.

FACE TO FACE WITH PIRATES
For Viking warriors, glory in battle was everything, and the ferocity of their attacks became legendary. The wild appearance of the bearded Norsemen fueled their barbarous reputation. This fierce-looking Viking head was carved on the side of a wagon.

BROADSWORD
Viking raiders attacked with broad, slashing swords.

Steering oar

Handle of wood or bone has rotted away

HEADS YOU LOSE

After a career spent menacing ships in the North Sea, the German pirate Klein Henszlein came to a grisly end. In 1573, he and his entire crew were beheaded in a mass execution in the center of Hamburg. The sword-wielding executioner flicked off their 33 heads so quickly, he was soon standing ankle deep in the pirates' blood. Displayed in a row, the heads warned others not to take up the pirate trade.

ON THE RIGHT VANE

The Vikings were expert mariners and navigators. Mounted on the prow of a ship, this beautiful golden weather vane indicated wind direction. When crossing the open sea, the Vikings used the sun and stars to guide them.

Lion points away from the wind

Bright gilding glittered impressively in the sun

SHIP SHAPE

The Vikings were master shipbuilders. Their later longboats were strengthened with keels to prevent them from breaking up in a strong sea swell, enabling them to cross the open ocean while other mariners hugged the coastline. Viking boats were also fast and easy to steer. Once by foreign shores, the shallow-keeled warships could land almost anywhere. This combination of factors made Viking raids particularly devastating – warships appeared as if from nowhere, and warriors stormed ashore with lightning speed.

Big, rectangular sail for use in the open sea

THE MAD DOG'S MASTER

Störtebeker, left, was the plague of the Baltic in the 14th century. To join his crew, aspiring pirates had to drink a huge beaker of beer in a single swallow. From this test, the pirate took his name, which means "a-beaker-at-a-gulp." When Störtebeker was finally caught, the mast of his ship, *The Mad Dog*, was said to have a core of pure gold.

Prow shaped like a snake's head

TO GO A-VIKING

The Scandinavian word *viking* means "going on an overseas raid." Raiding parties of up to 50 warriors were carried in Viking longboats. To intimidate their victims, the Vikings decorated their boats with shields and later ornamented them with gold and silver.

Oars for rowing into coastal waters and rivers

Keel

The Barbary Coast

EUROPEAN CRUSADERS CALLED THEIR Muslim opponents "barbarians," so the Islamic sea rovers became known as Barbary (barbarian) corsairs. The Barbary corsairs first set sail from the southern coast of the Mediterranean, which became known as the Barbary Coast. This was at the time of the Crusades, the holy wars between the Christians and Muslims that began at the end of the 11th century. In their sleek, fast galleys, the Barbary corsairs attacked trade vessels from Venice and Genoa in search of their preferred booty – men who could be sold as slaves. If corsairs boarded a Christian ship, the crew members might be stripped of their clothes and belongings. Moments later, they would be manning the oars of the corsairs' ship and changing course, for a life of slavery in an African port. In ferocious battles, Barbary corsairs rammed ships bound for the Crusades, and captured the wealthy Christian knights on board. The most famous corsairs were feared throughout Europe. Their exploits made them heroes in the Islamic world.

North African coast, home of the first barbary Corsairs

THE BARBARY COAST

Muslim Arabs took over North Africa in the 7th century. The Barbarossas fought off the Spanish in the 16th century, leading to rule by the Turks. A "Dey" or "Bey" (local prince) controlled each city-state. On this map, green represents the Christian-controlled area, beige the Muslim Ottoman Empire.

THE BARBAROSSA BROTHERS

Europeans nicknamed two 16th-century Barbary pirates, Aruj and Kheir-ed-Din, "the Barbarossa Brothers" because of their red beards. Aruj was killed in 1518, but his brother led Muslim resistance to Spanish attacks so successfully that in 1530 he won the regency (command) of the city of Algiers, Algeria. He died in 1546, greatly respected even by his enemies.

TURNING TURK

Sir Francis Verney (1584–1615; left) was one of a number of Europeans who "turned Turk" and joined the corsairs. Such men were welcomed because of their maritime skills. They paid taxes on their booty to the Barbary princes, who in turn protected them from revenge attacks. These Christian renegades sometimes adopted the Muslim faith of their new masters.

Verney's richly embroidered hat

Plush cloak was for everyday wear

Sleek Barbary galleys were capable of a speed of 9 knots (10 mph/16 kmph) over short distances

SEA BATTLE

The Barbary corsairs used slaves to power their sleek ships, but the slaves did not do any of the fighting. Muslim Janissaries – well-trained and highly disciplined professional soldiers – provided the military muscle. When a Barbary galley drew alongside its victim, as many as 100 Janissaries swarmed aboard the Christian vessel and overpowered the crew. This method of attack was very successful for the Barbary corsairs. Many Christian ships did not stand a chance.

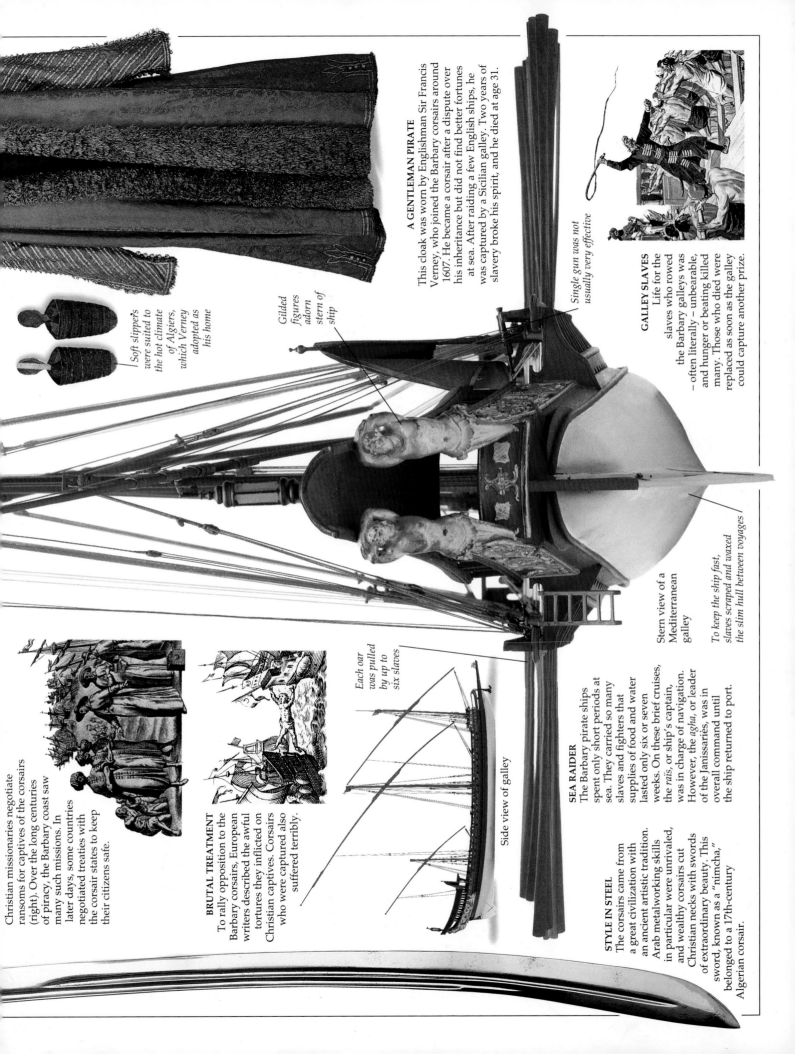

A GENTLEMAN PIRATE

This cloak was worn by Englishman Sir Francis Verney, who joined the Barbary corsairs around 1607. He became a corsair after a dispute over his inheritance but did not find better fortunes at sea. After raiding a few English ships, he was captured by a Sicilian galley. Two years of slavery broke his spirit, and he died at age 31.

Soft slippers were suited to the hot climate of Algiers, which Verney adopted as his home

Gilded figures adorn stern of ship

Single gun was not usually very effective

GALLEY SLAVES

Life for the slaves who rowed the Barbary galleys was – often literally – unbearable, and hunger or beating killed many. Those who died were replaced as soon as the galley could capture another prize.

Stern view of a Mediterranean galley

To keep the ship fast, slaves scraped and waxed the slim hull between voyages

Christian missionaries negotiate ransoms for captives of the corsairs (right). Over the long centuries of piracy, the Barbary coast saw many such missions. In later days, some countries negotiated treaties with the corsair states to keep their citizens safe.

BRUTAL TREATMENT

To rally opposition to the Barbary corsairs, European writers described the awful tortures they inflicted on Christian captives. Corsairs who were captured also suffered terribly.

Each oar was pulled by up to six slaves

Side view of galley

STYLE IN STEEL

The corsairs came from a great civilization with an ancient artistic tradition. Arab metalworking skills in particular were unrivaled, and wealthy corsairs cut Christian necks with swords of extraordinary beauty. This sword, known as a "nimcha," belonged to a 17th-century Algerian corsair.

SEA RAIDER

The Barbary pirate ships spent only short periods at sea. They carried so many slaves and fighters that supplies of food and water lasted only six or seven weeks. On these brief cruises, the *raïs*, or ship's captain, was in charge of navigation. However, the *agha*, or leader of the Janissaries, was in overall command until the ship returned to port.

The corsairs of Malta

DRIVEN BY GOD AND BY GOLD, the corsairs of Malta led the fight against the Barbary corsairs. With the Knights of Malta as their patrons, the corsairs waged a sea campaign against the "heathens" of Islam from their small island. When the Knights themselves captained the vessels, religious zeal was paramount, but as time went on, commerce crept in. The Knights still financed and organized the raids against their Barbary enemies, but for the Maltese, Corsicans, and French who crewed the galleys, the spoils of piracy became the main lure. The corsairs brought great wealth to Malta until the 1680s, when treaties between the European and Barbary powers led to a gradual decline in Mediterranean piracy.

EMBARKING FOR THE HOLY LAND
The Knights of the Order of St. John were formed in the early years of the Crusades to defend Jerusalem against attacks by Islamic forces. They also created hospitals to care for the Crusaders. This miniature shows Crusaders loading ships for the journey to the Holy Land. In 1530 they were given the island of Malta and became known as the Knights of Malta.

A carrack, forerunner of the galleon

A BOAT ON A BOTTLE
The Maltese galley fleet grew in size until the 1660s, when it numbered up to 30 carracks, such as the one pictured on this pharmacy jar. At this time, the corsair trade employed as much as a third of the Maltese population.

THE SIEGE OF MALTA
In 1565 the Knights of Malta had their greatest triumph against the Muslims when a fleet of the Ottoman Empire laid siege to Malta. The Knights were outnumbered five to one, but fought back bravely from inside their fort on Malta's northeast coast. When Spanish reinforcements arrived, the Ottoman fighters had to retreat. Six years later, the Knights fought again at the sea battle of Lepanto. Christian victory there finally ended Ottoman sea power in the Mediterranean.

CHRISTIAN GALLEY
The corsairs of Malta sailed similar galleys to their Muslim adversaries. However, the Christian galleys had two large sails instead of one, fewer oars, and more guns. The naked slaves at the oars were Muslims, and probably suffered a worse fate than their counterparts at the oars of the Barbary galleys. A French officer observed: "Many of the galley slaves have not room to sleep full length, for they put seven men on one bench [that is] ten feet long by four broad [3 m by 1.2 m]." This model represents a galley of the Knights of Malta c.1770, but the design had hardly changed since the 16th century.

Yard could be lowered onto the deck when the sail was not required

Lateen sail – a narrow, triangular sail attached to a long yard

Raised forecastle allowed the Maltese corsairs to jump down onto the lower decks of the Barbary galleys

Ram for smashing into enemy boats

Mizzen sail, introduced in 1700s

Sleek, narrow hull moved quickly through the water

Oars were the main means of propulsion

Wooden grip covered in leather and wrapped in wire

Cup-shaped handguard

Tiny Maltese crosses decorate the blade

19th-century sword is in the style of the Maltese rapiers of the 17th century

RAPIER
When Maltese corsairs stormed a ship, they fought with swords similar to this cup-hilt rapier. In their left hands, they may have carried daggers to fend off the sword thrusts of their Barbary opponents.

Upturned rim gave the Knight a clear view

HEADSTRONG KNIGHTS
Fighting Knights wore crested helmets called morions that were shaped to deflect blows. Even though they were heavy, a morion would not save a Knight from a direct hit by a Barbary musket ball.

Huge curled perukes, wigs that became fashionable around the time of the siege

MALTESE CROSS
In battle and in command of their galleys, the Knights of the Order of St. John (who became known as the Knights of Malta) wore the eight-pointed cross of Malta, shown here on the breastplate of a knight from the early 1700s. The present-day flag of Malta takes its colors from the white cross and red background.

ITALIAN BUT OUT OF FASHION
The Knights' round Italian targe (target) shields were quite plain for the time. This one has a subtly engraved surface, but the fashion was for more ornate styles.

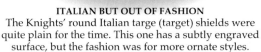

Celebratory medal with Cotoner's portrait

HEAVY METAL
Armed to the teeth against their Muslim foes, the Knights of Malta saw themselves as soldiers of the Christian faith. This breastplate was worn for fighting both on land and at sea.

GRAND MASTER OF THE BUILDERS
After the great siege, the Knights of Malta began to strengthen their fortress against further attacks by their Barbary enemies. The building program lasted for more than a century. Nicolas Cotoner was the Knights' Grand Master when they finished the building work.

The privateers

"KNOW YE THAT WE HAVE GRANTED and given license… to Adam Robernolt and William le Sauvage. . . to annoy our enemies at sea or by land. . . so that they shall share with us half of all their gain." With these words the English king Henry III issued one of the first letters of marque in 1243. Virtually a pirate's license, the letter was convenient for all concerned – the ship's crew was given the right to plunder without punishment, and the king acquired a free man-of-war, or battleship, as well as a share of the booty. At first such ships were called "private men-of-war," but in the course of time, they and their crews became known as privateers. Between the 16th and 18th centuries, privateering flourished as European nations fought each other in costly wars. Privateers were supposed to attack only enemy shipping, but many found ways to bend the rules.

ROYAL HONORS
The English queen Elizabeth I (1558–1603) honored the adventurer and privateer Francis Drake (1540–1596), whom she called her "pirate," with a knighthood in 1581. Drake's privateering had brought her great wealth – the equivalent of millions of dollars in modern currency.

OFFICIAL REPRISALS
English king Henry III (1216–1272) issued the first known letters of marque. There were two kinds. In wartime, the king issued general letters of marque authorizing privateers to attack enemy ships. In peacetime, merchants who had lost ships or cargoes to pirates could apply for a special letter of marque. This allowed them to attack ships of the pirates' nation to recover their loss.

PRIVATEER PROMOTER
English navigator Walter Raleigh (1522–1618) was greatly in favor of privateering, recognizing that it brought huge income to his country. He also promoted privateering for his own gain, equipping many privateers in the hope that he could finance a colony in Virginia on the proceeds.

THE PIRATE'S LICENSE
Letters of marque, such as this one issued by England's king George III (1760–1820), contained many restrictions. But corrupt shipowners could buy one, granting them license to plunder innocent merchant ships.

"HERE'S TO PLUNDER"
A prosperous privateer captain of the 18th century could afford to toast a new venture with a fine glass like this one. The engraving on the glass reads, "Success to the Duke of Cornwall Privateer."

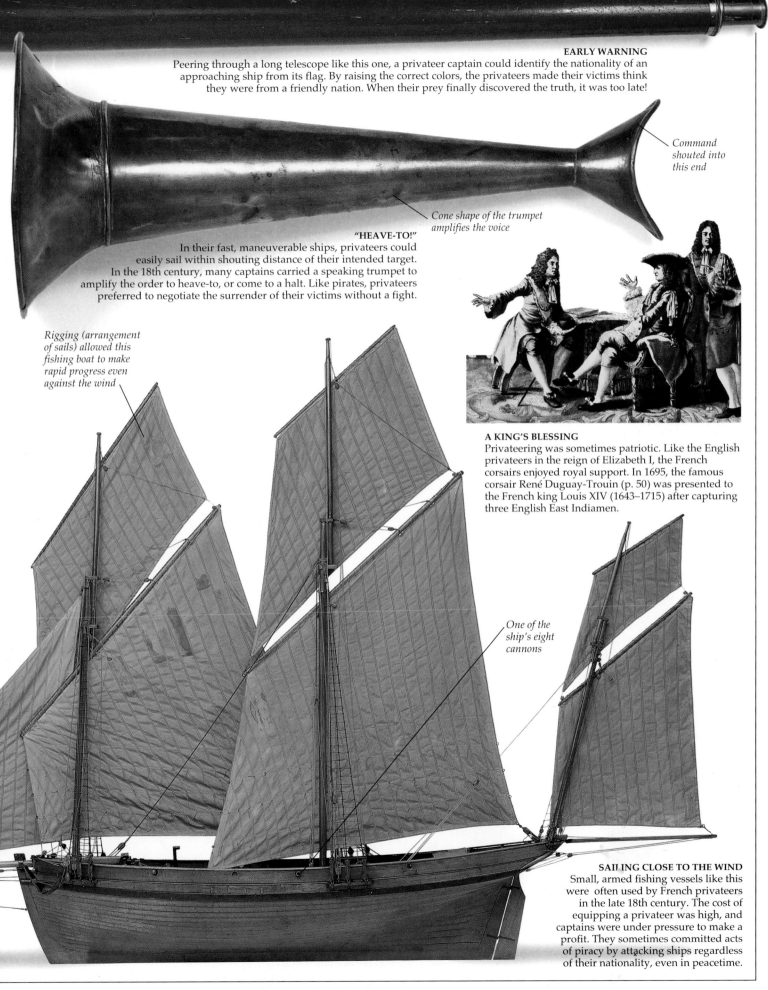

EARLY WARNING

Peering through a long telescope like this one, a privateer captain could identify the nationality of an approaching ship from its flag. By raising the correct colors, the privateers made their victims think they were from a friendly nation. When their prey finally discovered the truth, it was too late!

Command shouted into this end

Cone shape of the trumpet amplifies the voice

"HEAVE-TO!"

In their fast, maneuverable ships, privateers could easily sail within shouting distance of their intended target. In the 18th century, many captains carried a speaking trumpet to amplify the order to heave-to, or come to a halt. Like pirates, privateers preferred to negotiate the surrender of their victims without a fight.

Rigging (arrangement of sails) allowed this fishing boat to make rapid progress even against the wind

A KING'S BLESSING

Privateering was sometimes patriotic. Like the English privateers in the reign of Elizabeth I, the French corsairs enjoyed royal support. In 1695, the famous corsair René Duguay-Trouin (p. 50) was presented to the French king Louis XIV (1643–1715) after capturing three English East Indiamen.

One of the ship's eight cannons

SAILING CLOSE TO THE WIND

Small, armed fishing vessels like this were often used by French privateers in the late 18th century. The cost of equipping a privateer was high, and captains were under pressure to make a profit. They sometimes committed acts of piracy by attacking ships regardless of their nationality, even in peacetime.

The Spanish Main

A Spanish galleon

FAMED IN PIRATE LEGEND, the Spanish Main lured adventurers and pirates with the promise of untold riches. The Spanish Main was Spain's empire in the "New World" of North and South America. After Christopher Columbus landed on an island in the Caribbean in 1492, the New World (or Western Hemisphere) was found to contain treasures beyond the Europeans' wildest dreams. Spanish conquistadors, or conquerors, ruthlessly plundered the wealth of the Aztec and Inca nations of Mexico and Peru, and throughout the 16th and 17th centuries, vast quantities of gold and silver were shipped back to Europe. The Spanish treasure ships soon attracted the attention of privateers and pirates eager for a share of the booty, prompting the beginning of piracy on the Spanish Main.

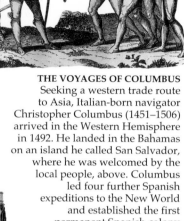

THE VOYAGES OF COLUMBUS
Seeking a western trade route to Asia, Italian-born navigator Christopher Columbus (1451–1506) arrived in the Western Hemisphere in 1492. He landed in the Bahamas on an island he called San Salvador, where he was welcomed by the local people, above. Columbus led four further Spanish expeditions to the New World and established the first permanent Spanish colony on the Caribbean island of Hispaniola (pp. 26–27).

Aztec treasure loaded at Veracruz

Treasure ships rendezvous at Havana for return to Europe

Mexico

Atlantic Ocean

San Salvador

Cuba

Jamaica

Hispaniola

Pacific Ocean

Peru

Inca treasure loaded at Nombre de Dios

Panama

High up in the crow's nest, the ship's lookout kept watch for pirates

High forecastle

IN THE MAIN
The term "Spanish Main" originally meant the parts of the Central and South American mainlands, from Mexico to Peru, taken by Spain. Later it came to include the islands and waters of the Caribbean.

This 1491 globe has a gap where the Americas ought to be

OLD WORLD
Made before 1492, this early globe does not include the New World. It shows how Columbus thought he could find a route to Asia by sailing across the Atlantic.

TREASURE SHIP
New World treasure was carried back to Europe in Spanish galleons. A galleon usually had a crew of about 200 men and an armament of up to 60 cannons. Although well built, with a strong wooden hull and powerful rig, these great ships were difficult to maneuver, and in spite of their guns, galleons often proved no match for smaller, swifter pirate vessels. Therefore, as a safeguard, the treasure ships crossed the Atlantic in vast convoys of up to 100 vessels.

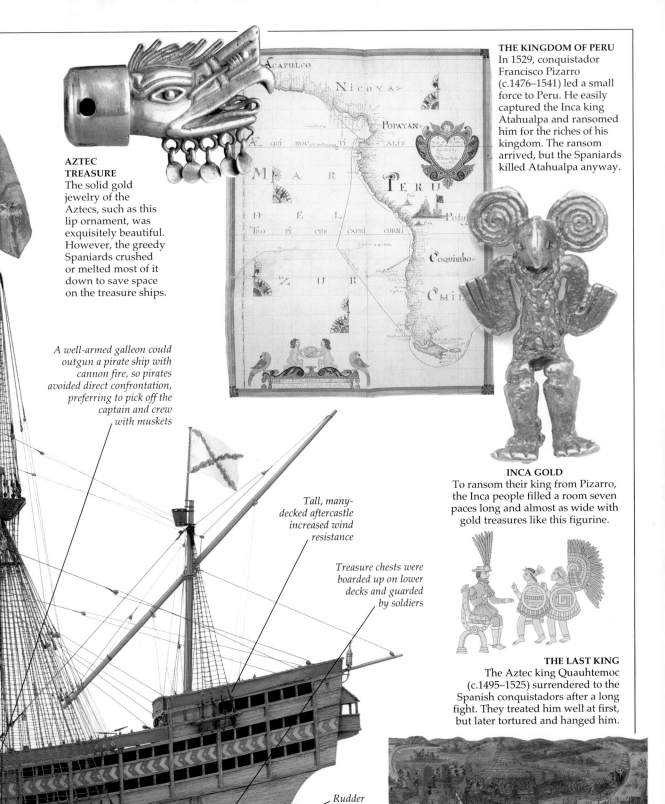

Equipped with a large, square sail on each mainmast, a galleon sailed well with the wind behind it, but was slow sailing upwind

AZTEC TREASURE
The solid gold jewelry of the Aztecs, such as this lip ornament, was exquisitely beautiful. However, the greedy Spaniards crushed or melted most of it down to save space on the treasure ships.

A well-armed galleon could outgun a pirate ship with cannon fire, so pirates avoided direct confrontation, preferring to pick off the captain and crew with muskets

Tall, many-decked aftercastle increased wind resistance

Treasure chests were boarded up on lower decks and guarded by soldiers

Rudder

Hull floated high in the water because the galleon had to load and unload in shallow rivers and bays

THE KINGDOM OF PERU
In 1529, conquistador Francisco Pizarro (c.1476–1541) led a small force to Peru. He easily captured the Inca king Atahualpa and ransomed him for the riches of his kingdom. The ransom arrived, but the Spaniards killed Atahualpa anyway.

INCA GOLD
To ransom their king from Pizarro, the Inca people filled a room seven paces long and almost as wide with gold treasures like this figurine.

THE LAST KING
The Aztec king Quauhtemoc (c.1495–1525) surrendered to the Spanish conquistadors after a long fight. They treated him well at first, but later tortured and hanged him.

A NATION FALLS
This painting shows the Spanish army of Hernán Cortés (1485–1547) defeating the Aztecs in Mexico. In their lust for gold, the conquistadors completely destroyed the ancient American civilizations of the Aztecs and Incas.

New World privateers

SILVER SOURCE
The Spanish colonists at first enslaved local people to work the silver mines in the New World. But locals proved unwilling – many died from beatings intended to drive them to work – so the Spanish brought in African slaves.

T REASURE FROM THE Spanish Main amazed the people of 16th-century Europe. The Spanish writer Bernal Díaz marveled at items like a gold disk "in the shape of the sun, as big as a cartwheel." Soon Spain's many enemies were setting sail to get a share of this rich booty. Among the first on the scene were the French; the English privateers, led by Francis Drake and John Hawkins, soon followed. Their success encouraged many adventurers to make trips to the Main. Desperate to return home rich, some crossed the thin line between privateering and piracy, attacking ships of any nation.

NARROWS NAVIGATOR
French ships made the first successful raids on the Spanish treasure galleons. Genoese navigator Giovanni da Verrazano (c.1485–c.1528), sailing for the French, took three Spanish ships in 1522. Two were laden with Mexican treasure; the third carried sugar, hides, and pearls. Verrazano is better known for the discovery (in 1524) of New York Bay, and the narrows there is named for him.

ATTACKING A TREASURE SHIP
Spanish treasure ships were most vulnerable to attack in the early stages of their voyages. Privateers knew the ships had to head north from the Caribbean to find a favorable wind before returning to Spain. So, waiting off the North American coast, the privateers could take the Spanish by surprise.

PIECES OF EIGHT
From New World gold and silver, the Spanish minted doubloons and pieces of eight, which became the currency of later pirates.

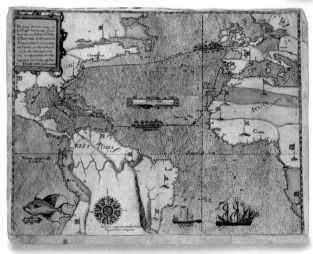

DRAKE'S 1585 CRUISE
The exploits of English privateer and pirate Francis Drake (c.1540–96) made him a popular hero in his home country. The Spanish had attacked his ship in 1568, and the incident left Drake with a hatred for Spain. His 1585–86 voyage marked on the map above became known as Drake's "Descent on the Indies." He attacked the port of Vigo in Spain, then crossed the Atlantic to raid Spanish colonies in the New World.

WARNING BEAT
Drake's successful 1588 defense of England against the Spanish Armada, or invasion fleet, further enhanced his reputation as a nautical hero. The drum he carried on board his many voyages is still preserved and is said to sound an eerie beat when England is in danger.

PRIVATEER SHIP
Early privateers sailed in tiny ships, such as 50- to 100-ton barks with crews of just 40 or 50. Later, though, they used larger merchant ships of 100–300 tons, similar to this one from around 1588. The ships were very crowded because they carried extra crews to sail any captured prize ships.

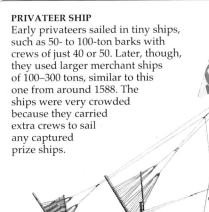

PIRATES OR PRIVATEERS?
English adventurers Thomas Cavendish (c.1555–c.1592), Drake, and Hawkins were celebrated privateers. Though each held letters of marque or reprisal, Cavendish was the only one who confined his raids to wartime. The Spanish and other nationalities regarded all three as pirates.

SANTA DOMINGO
Drake's raid on the Spanish capital in the New World, Santa Domingo in Hispaniola, was a disappointment. Though still a large settlement, the town was declining, and Drake could only get a small ransom. His later raid on Cartagena (in present-day Colombia) was a huge success.

Lower, sleeker shape made privateers' ships more maneuverable than the Spanish galleons

Cannon balls splintered timber and brought down sails

GALLEON BASHER
Improvements in maritime cannons gave privateers a considerable advantage over their Spanish foes. The traditional Spanish fighting tactic was to board the enemy vessel and then fight as in a land battle. But by Drake's time, a cannon like this one could throw a 50-lb (20-kg) ball as much as 1 mi (1.5 km), making boarding impossible as an attack or defense strategy.

Navigation and maps

SUCCESS FOR PIRATES on the Spanish Main (p. 20) meant outwitting, out-sailing, and out-fighting the chosen prey, but how did pirates find their victims? Navigation was primitive. Pirates had to position their ships along the routes taken by Spanish treasure ships using a mixture of knowledge, common sense, and good luck. They could estimate latitude quite accurately by measuring the position of the sun, but judging longitude was more difficult. Besides a compass, the most vital navigational aid available to a pirate captain was a chart. Spanish ships had surveyed much of the New World coast in the early 16th century, and their detailed charts were valuable prizes. With a stolen Spanish chart, pirates and buccaneers could plunder the riches of new areas of coastline.

This page of the waggoner shows the coastline around Panama

A description of the sea coast

A WAGGONER OF THE SOUTH SEA
Pirates called books of charts "waggoners." This waggoner of the Pacific coast of South America was seized from the Spanish by the buccaneer Bartholomew Sharp. In 1681, he wrote in his journal: "I took a Spanish manuscript of prodigious value – it describes all the ports, roads, harbours, bays, sands, rocks and rising of the land, and instructions how to work a ship into any port or harbour." English mapmaker William Hack made this copy in 1685.

Dividers and chart
Globe
Vellum chart
Cross-staff
Astrolabe

SEA ARTISTS AT WORK
Pirates called skilled navigators "sea artists"; this fanciful illustration shows a group of them with the tools of their trade. In ideal conditions they could judge distance to within about 1.3 m (2 km), but on the deck of a pitching ship navigation was far less precise.

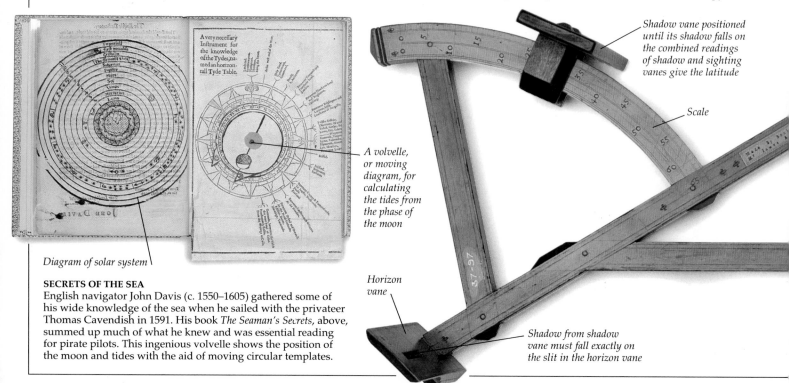

A volvelle, or moving diagram, for calculating the tides from the phase of the moon

Diagram of solar system

SECRETS OF THE SEA
English navigator John Davis (c. 1550–1605) gathered some of his wide knowledge of the sea when he sailed with the privateer Thomas Cavendish in 1591. His book *The Seaman's Secrets*, above, summed up much of what he knew and was essential reading for pirate pilots. This ingenious volvelle shows the position of the moon and tides with the aid of moving circular templates.

Shadow vane positioned until its shadow falls on the combined readings of shadow and sighting vanes give the latitude

Scale

Horizon vane

Shadow from shadow vane must fall exactly on the slit in the horizon vane

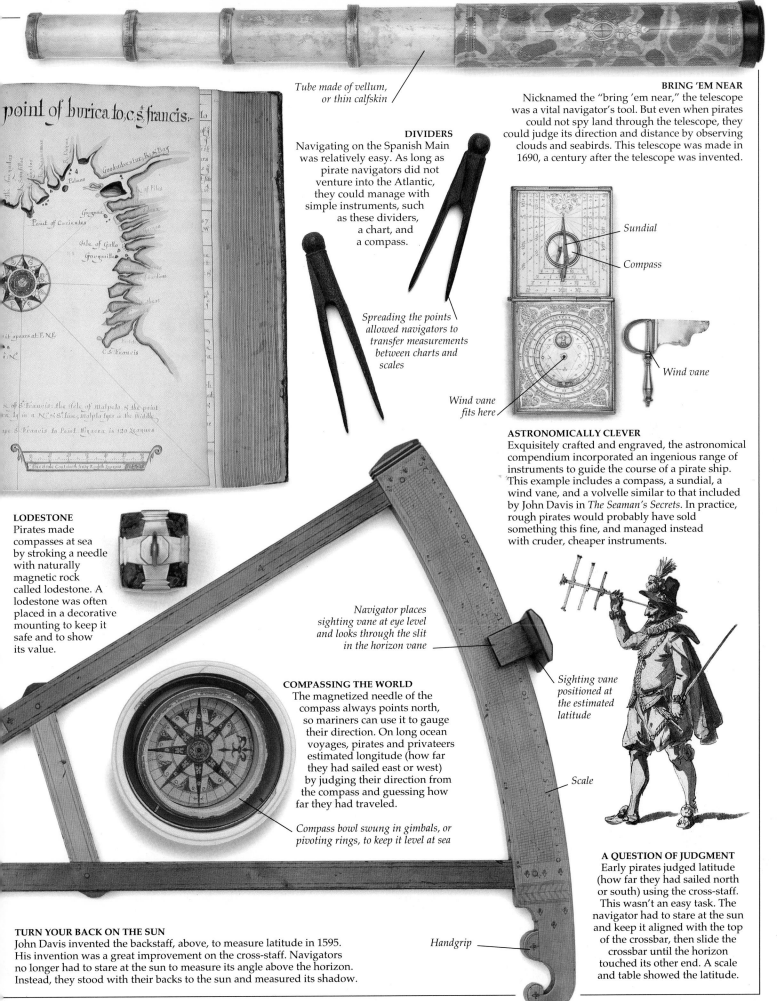

point of burica to c.s. francis:-

BRING 'EM NEAR
Nicknamed the "bring 'em near," the telescope was a vital navigator's tool. But even when pirates could not spy land through the telescope, they could judge its direction and distance by observing clouds and seabirds. This telescope was made in 1690, a century after the telescope was invented.

Tube made of vellum, or thin calfskin

DIVIDERS
Navigating on the Spanish Main was relatively easy. As long as pirate navigators did not venture into the Atlantic, they could manage with simple instruments, such as these dividers, a chart, and a compass.

Sundial

Compass

Spreading the points allowed navigators to transfer measurements between charts and scales

Wind vane

Wind vane fits here

ASTRONOMICALLY CLEVER
Exquisitely crafted and engraved, the astronomical compendium incorporated an ingenious range of instruments to guide the course of a pirate ship. This example includes a compass, a sundial, a wind vane, and a volvelle similar to that included by John Davis in *The Seaman's Secrets*. In practice, rough pirates would probably have sold something this fine, and managed instead with cruder, cheaper instruments.

LODESTONE
Pirates made compasses at sea by stroking a needle with naturally magnetic rock called lodestone. A lodestone was often placed in a decorative mounting to keep it safe and to show its value.

Navigator places sighting vane at eye level and looks through the slit in the horizon vane

Sighting vane positioned at the estimated latitude

COMPASSING THE WORLD
The magnetized needle of the compass always points north, so mariners can use it to gauge their direction. On long ocean voyages, pirates and privateers estimated longitude (how far they had sailed east or west) by judging their direction from the compass and guessing how far they had traveled.

Scale

Compass bowl swung in gimbals, or pivoting rings, to keep it level at sea

A QUESTION OF JUDGMENT
Early pirates judged latitude (how far they had sailed north or south) using the cross-staff. This wasn't an easy task. The navigator had to stare at the sun and keep it aligned with the top of the crossbar, then slide the crossbar until the horizon touched its other end. A scale and table showed the latitude.

TURN YOUR BACK ON THE SUN
John Davis invented the backstaff, above, to measure latitude in 1595. His invention was a great improvement on the cross-staff. Navigators no longer had to stare at the sun to measure its angle above the horizon. Instead, they stood with their backs to the sun and measured its shadow.

Handgrip

The buccaneers

ENGLAND'S KING, James I, opened a bloody chapter in the history of the Spanish Main (p. 20) in 1603. To end the chaos of privateering raids in the Caribbean, he withdrew all letters of marque (p. 18). This had disastrous consequences. Bands of lawless buccaneers soon replaced the privateers. Originally hunters from the island of Hispaniola, the buccaneers banded together into a loyal brotherhood when the hated Spanish tried to drive them out. They began by attacking small Spanish ships, then went after bigger prizes. Convicts, outlaws, and escaped slaves swelled their numbers. The buccaneers obeyed no laws except their own, and their leaders maintained discipline with horrible acts of cruelty. However, some, such as Henry Morgan, fought for fame and glory and became heroes.

BLOODY BUCCANEERS
The original buccaneers lived by supplying meat, fat, and hides to passing ships. They hunted pigs and cattle that had bred rapidly when Spanish settlers left the island of Hispaniola. Buccaneers had a wild reputation. They dressed in uncured hides and were stinking and bloody from their trade.

Tortuga

AN EARLY BARBECUE
The Arawak Indians taught the buccaneers to cure meat in *boucans*, or smokehouses, like this one. These *boucans* gave the "boucaniers" their name.

A BUCCANEERING JOURNAL
Surgeon Basil Ringrose (1653–86) sailed with the buccaneer Bartholomew Sharp on his expedition of 1680–82 along the Pacific coast of South America. His detailed journal of the voyage is one of the main sources of knowledge of buccaneering life.

Isle à Vache

17th-century mariner's chart of Hispaniola (present-day Haiti and Dominican Republic)

CRUEL AND BLOODTHIRSTY CUTTHROATS
In the dangerous waters of the Spanish Main, life was cheap and the torture of prisoners commonplace. Nevertheless, the cruelty of the buccaneers became legendary. L'Ollonais, above, tortured his victims with grisly originality. On one occasion, he cut out the heart of a Spanish prisoner and stuffed it into the mouth of another.

Sword and sheath reputedly carried by one of Morgan's buccaneers in 1670

FRANCIS L'OLLONAIS
The cruelest of a cruel gang, French buccaneer L'Ollonais struck fear into the Spanish, who preferred to die, rather than give in to the buccaneer. He tortured those he captured, then cut them to pieces.

ROCK BRAZILIANO
Nicknamed for his long exile in Brazil, this "brutish and foolish" drunkard loathed the Spanish. He once spit-roasted two Spanish farmers alive because they would not give him their pigs for food.

GREAT ESCAPE
Ingenious and daring, Bartholomew the Portuguese captured valuable prizes but was caught a few days later. He could not swim, but escaped from a prison ship by using wine jars for floats.

Chart mounted on hinged oak "plats" to protect it at sea

HISPANOLA

SIR HENRY MORGAN
The most famous of the buccaneers, Welshman Henry Morgan (c.1635–88) was a natural leader. He was probably just as cruel as other buccaneers, but his daring attacks on Spanish colonies, most notably Panama, won him an English knighthood and the governorship of Jamaica.

Isla Saona

THE BUCCANEER ISLAND
As hunters, the buccaneers lived peacefully on Hispaniola, left, until the Spanish attacked them and destroyed the animals they lived on. The buccaneers formed the "Brotherhood of the Coast" to defend themselves, and some moved to Tortuga, where they could prey on Spanish ships. The arrival of French garrisons later dispersed some of the brotherhood to Isle à Vache and Isla Saona.

THE ORIGIN OF THE CUTLASS
According to legend, buccaneers invented the cutlass. The long knives used by the original buccaneers to butcher meat for the *boucan* evolved into the famous short sword used by all seamen.

A BRUTAL ATTACK
Morgan carried out his raids on Spanish colonies with military discipline but without mercy. In 1668, his 800 men defeated the soldiers of Puerto Príncipe on Cuba, right. They forced the men of the town to surrender by threatening to tear their wives and children to pieces. Imprisoned in churches, the people starved while the buccaneers pillaged their possessions.

Weapons

BOOM! WITH A DEAFENING EXPLOSION and a puff of smoke, a pirate cannon signals the attack. Crack! A well-aimed musket ball catches the helmsman, but the ship careers on, out of control. Crash! The mainsail tumbles to the deck as the boarding pirates chop through the sail lifts. After such a dramatic show of force, most sailors were reluctant to challenge the pirates who rushed on board, brandishing weapons and yelling terrifying threats. Few crews put up a fight. Those who did faced the razor-sharp cutlasses of seasoned cutthroats. The only way to repel a pirate attack successfully was to avoid a pitched battle. Brave crew members barricaded themselves into the strongest part of the ship and fought back courageously with guns and also homemade bombs.

FLYING CANNON BALLS
Cannons rarely sank a ship, but inside the hull the impact of the iron balls created a whirlwind of deadly wooden splinters. Chain shot (two balls chained together and aimed high) took down masts, sails, and rigging to disable a vessel.

CUTTHROAT CUTLASS
In the 17th and 18th centuries, the cutlass was favored by all fighting men at sea. Its short, broad blade was the ideal weapon for hand-to-hand fighting on board a ship – a longer sword would be easily tangled in the rigging.

Short blade was easy to wield on a crowded deck

Firing mechanism, or lock

Wooden stock

MUSKETOON
The short barrel of the musketoon limited its accuracy, so pirates would have used this gun only when they were close to their victims. Like the longer musket, it was fired from the shoulder, but the short barrel made the musketoon easier to handle on a cramped, pitching deck.

Patch and musket ball

Patch boxes were often fixed to a belt

Cock holds flint, which strikes frizzen, making sparks

Frizzen

Sparks ignite powder in priming pan

FLINTLOCK PISTOL
Light and portable, the pistol was the pirate's favorite weapon for boarding a ship. However, sea air sometimes dampened the powder, so that the gun misfired and went off with a quiet "flash in the pan". Reloading was so slow that pirates often didn't bother, preferring to use the gun's butt as a club.

Brass-covered butt could be used as a club

Ramrod for pushing the ball and patch into the barrel

Cock

Flint

PATCH BOXES
To keep a musket ball from rolling out of a loaded gun, pirates wrapped the ball in a patch of cloth to make it fit tightly in the barrel. Patches were stored in patch boxes.

MARKSMAN'S MUSKET
With a long musket, a pirate marksman could take out the helmsman of a ship from a distance. Rifling, or spiral grooving cut inside the musket barrel, spun the musket ball so that it flew in a straight line. This improved accuracy, but a marksman still needed calm seas for careful aiming.

Butt rests against the shoulder

Trigger

Trigger guard

WHIRLING CUTLASSES
Infamous pirate Blackbeard (pp.30–31), left, fought like a devil with both pistol and cutlass. In his last fight, Captain Johnson (p. 61) tells how Blackbeard: "stood his ground, and fought with great fury till he received five and twenty wounds."

AX ATTACK
Pirates used axes to help climb the high wooden sides of larger vessels they boarded. Once on deck, the ax brought down the sails – a single blow could cut through ropes as thick as a man's arm.

NO MERCY
If pirates' victims resisted attack, none would be spared in the fight that followed. Though this 19th-century print possibly exaggerates the cold-blooded brutality of the pirates, even women received no mercy.

COMING ABOARD!
The notorious Barbary corsair, Dragut Rais, right, was known as a brave fighter. Here, he is shown storming aboard a ship armed with a pirate's favored weapons: pistols, short sword, and ax.

Muzzle

Brass barrel

DAGGERS DRAWN
The dagger was small enough for a pirate to conceal under clothing in a surprise attack, and was lethal on the lower deck, where there was no space to swing a sword.

FIGHT TO THE DEATH
Battles between Mediterranean pirates in the 16th and 17th centuries were especially ferocious, because they pitted two great religions against each other. Christian forces – Greek corsairs in this picture – fought not just for booty, but also because they believed they had God on their side. Their Ottoman opponents were Muslims, and believed the same. This 19th-century engraving vividly captures the no-holds-barred nature of their conflict.

GREAT BALLS OF FIRE
Thrown from the high forecastle of a pirate ship, a homemade grenade could start a fire that spread quickly. More often, a smoldering mixture of tar and rags filled the bomb, creating a smoke screen of confusion and panic.

BAREFOOT BARBS
French corsairs sometimes tossed these vicious-looking caltrops, or crowsfeet, onto the deck of a ship they were boarding. Since sailors worked barefoot to avoid slipping on wet decks, the spikes could inflict terrible injuries if stepped on.

Spikes angled so that one always points up

BIG GUNS
Firing a cannon effectively required rigid discipline: even the best drilled navy gun teams needed two to five minutes to load and fire. Ill-disciplined pirate crews rarely managed more than one shot per gun before boarding.

Pirates of the Caribbean

HE WAS A STORYBOOK PIRATE with wild, staring eyes and a cruel streak; he wore lighted candles in his hair; he drank rum mixed with gunpowder; he twisted his beard in black ringlets around his ears. Was it surprising that Blackbeard terrified 18th-century mariners – and even his own crew? Blackbeard was typical of a new breed of pirates who succeeded the unruly buccaneers when their Caribbean island hosts threw them out at the end of the 17th century. Many former buccaneers worked as privateers during the wars of the early 18th century. When peace returned, the pirate ways of freedom and adventure still beckoned. Pirate ports blossomed in the Bahamas and on mainland America. A few ruffians sailed farther afield, all the way to the island of Madagascar in the Indian Ocean. But all these had become plain pirates, plundering ships of every flag and leaving a trail of terror behind them.

Edward Low plied his sword with awesome skill, using it to slaughter the crew of a Spanish man-of-war in 1723

BULLIES
Low's men could be as cruel as their captain. This picture shows one of Low's men shooting a Spanish prisoner.

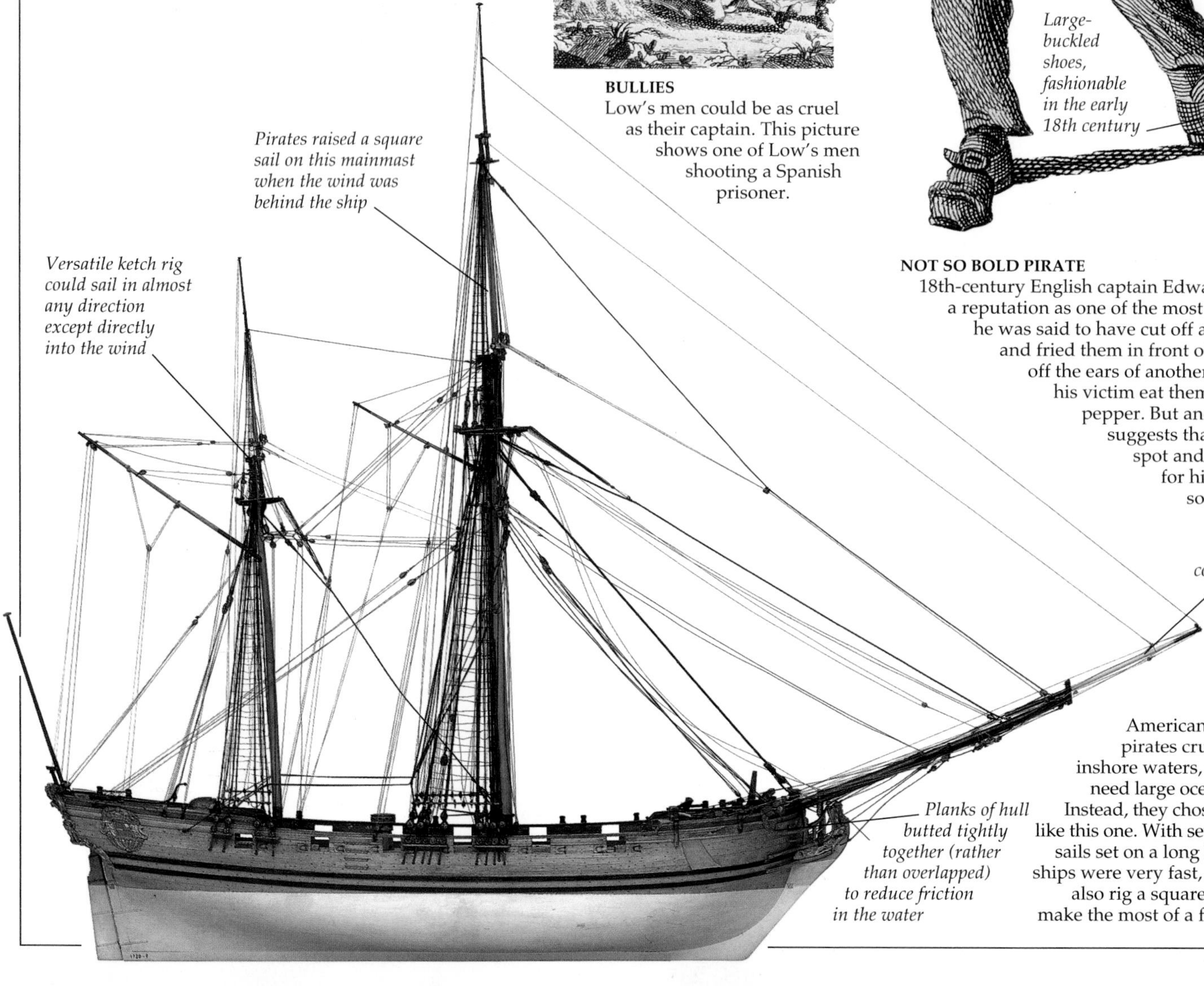

Large-buckled shoes, fashionable in the early 18th century

NOT SO BOLD PIRATE
18th-century English captain Edward Low had a reputation as one of the most cruel pirates: he was said to have cut off a man's lips and fried them in front of him; he cut off the ears of another and made his victim eat them with salt and pepper. But another account suggests that he had a soft spot and often wept for his orphan son in Boston.

Pirates raised a square sail on this mainmast when the wind was behind the ship

Versatile ketch rig could sail in almost any direction except directly into the wind

Bowsprit could be almost as long as the hull

SWIFT KETCH
American and Bahamian pirates cruised mainly on inshore waters, so they did not need large ocean-going ships. Instead, they chose small ketches like this one. With several triangular sails set on a long bowsprit, these ships were very fast, and they could also rig a square sail in order to make the most of a following wind.

Planks of hull butted tightly together (rather than overlapped) to reduce friction in the water

NEW GOVERNOR FOR NEW PROVIDENCE

The island of New Providence in the Bahamas briefly flourished as a pirate haven and lawless republic between 1715 and 1720. The pirate party ended with the arrival of a new governor, Woodes Rogers (1679–1732), from England. Rogers offered the pirates a pardon if they gave up their trade. He hanged eight who refused and eventually cleared the pirate's lair.

Smoldering lengths of hempen cord soaked in saltpeter produced thick black smoke around Blackbeard's head

RANSOM TOWN

Welcomed in nearby North Carolina, Blackbeard (?–1718) was feared in Charleston, South Carolina. In 1718, he blockaded the harbor. Then the pirate ransomed one of the town's council members and his four-year-old child in exchange for a chest of medicine.

Beard twisted into plaits

RELUCTANT STAR

Perhaps the most prolific pirate of all, Welshman Bartholomew Roberts, or Black Bart (1682–1722), was forced into piracy when his ship was captured in 1719. He went on to capture as many as 400 ships.

Maze of sandbars, marked on this old chart, ultimately trapped Blackbeard

OCRACOKE INLET

Ocracoke Island, part of the Outer Banks chain of islands that extends along the coast of North Carolina, was the scene of many pirate parties (p. 45). Blackbeard moored in its inlet, judging (incorrectly) that the shallow waters made him immune to attack.

Pushed into the belts that crossed his chest, Blackbeard carried six pistols

MYSTERIOUS MONSTER

Myth and truth about Blackbeard are inseparable. He is said to have had 14 wives, and almost as many names, including Drummond, Thatch, Tash, and (officially) Edward Teach. Details of his birth are obscure, but his death, after a reign of terror lasting two years, is well documented. He was slain at Ocracoke Inlet by a British navy crew in 1718.

END OF A SWEET AFFAIR

Until the 1690s, Jamaican planters valued the protection provided by buccaneers against Spanish attacks, although they still called their guardians "pirates." When pirates began raiding ships carrying Jamaican produce such as this sugarloaf, the unruly crews were no longer welcome.

Women pirates

MARY READ
English pirate Mary Read (1690–1720) found it easier to live her life dressed as a man. She fought in the English army and navy – disguised in men's clothes – and when Rackham's pirates captured her transatlantic ship, she joined them. Read's valor shamed the pirates she sailed with. During an attack, all but one hid while she and Anne Bonny fought. When they would not come out and "fight like men," Read shot the cowards.

PIRACY WAS A MAN'S WORLD, just like the 18th-century worlds of business, art, or politics. So women who dreamed of sailing the seas under the Jolly Roger had to become men, or at least dress, fight, drink, and swear like men. Most of those who succeeded escaped the notice of history – today we know only of those women who were unmasked. The bold exploits of female pirates Mary Read and Anne Bonny seem amazing, but they are not surprising. They form part of a long tradition of women adventurers who dressed as men to gain equal treatment. Like many of their female contemporaries, Read and Bonny lacked neither strength nor courage. Fighting fearlessly alongside each other in battle, this formidable duo daunted even the bravest of pirates and naval men.

THE TERRIBLE ALVILDA
One of the first female pirate captains was Alvilda, a Goth who came from southern Sweden, in the time before the Vikings. She went to sea with an all-woman crew to avoid an enforced marriage to Danish prince Alf.

A CUTLASS ABOVE THE REST
When a fellow pirate threatened her lover, Mary Read challenged him to a duel. She easily dispatched her foe by stabbing him with her cutlass.

Dashing red sash favored by pirates

PIRATE DRESS
Women were banned from most pirate ships, so Mary Read and Anne Bonny had to disguise themselves in clothes like these. Descriptions of the women's attire differ: one writer claimed they hid their identities from the crew up to the moment of their trial. But other eyewitnesses said that they wore men's clothes only for fighting.

CALICO JACK
From 1718, "Calico" Jack Rackham, left, and Anne Bonny were pirates and lovers in the Caribbean, later joined by Mary Read. All three were caught when Rackham's ship was surprised by a British navy sloop off Jamaica. Bonny and Read were the only members of the intoxicated crew brave enough to fend off the attack, but they too were captured. In 1720 the pirates were sentenced to death. As Rackham went to the gallows, Bonny told him, "Had you fought like a man, you need not have been hanged like a dog!"

Buckled leather shoe fashionable in the 18th century

Rugged calico trousers with bone buttons

A BRILLIANT DISGUISE?

The loose-fitting cut of the pirate jacket, below, fooled fellow pirates, but it couldn't completely conceal the feminine shapes of Read and Bonny from the sharp eyes of another woman. When they attacked a merchant ship, female passenger Dorothy Thomas recalled, "By the largeness of their breasts, I believed them to be women."

Linen cravat to keep the neck warm

Loose-fitting blue jacket

Leather warrior's baldric, or belt, for holding a cutlass

Blue-and-white checked sailor's shirt made of linen

WIELDING AN AXE

Portraits of Anne Bonny and Mary Read show them armed with hefty boarding axes like this one. The fact that they could swing these heavy tools suggests they had the strength to tackle any task on board ship.

Turbanlike headgear worn by pirates and other seafarers

Pirate queen Ching Shih battles with dagger and cutlass

CHING SHIH

In the early 19th century, a huge pirate fleet terrorized the China Sea. Its commander was the brilliant female pirate Ching Shih. Female sea captains weren't unusual, but the vastness of Ching Shih's empire was – she controlled 1,800 ships and about 80,000 pirates.

DAGGERS DRAWN

Charlotte de Berry's life as a pirate began when she led a mutiny against a cruel captain who had assaulted her. She cut off the captain's head with a sharp dagger.

Flintlock pistol

CHARLOTTE DE BERRY

Born in England in 1636, Charlotte de Berry, right, grew up dreaming of a life at sea. Dressed as a man, she followed her husband into the navy. Later, forced aboard an Africa-bound vessel, de Berry led a mutiny and took over the ship. Under her command, the crew became pirates and cruised the African coast capturing gold ships.

ANNE BONNY

When Anne Bonny, right, met the pirate Jack Rackham, she left her sailor husband to take up a life of piracy dressed as a man. Bonny accidentally fell in love with Mary Read when Read, also in male disguise, joined Rackham's crew. Read told Bonny her secret and the pair became firm friends. When Rackham's pirates were captured, the two women escaped the death penalty since both were pregnant.

The Jolly Roger

GRAVE EXAMPLE
Pirates probably borrowed their symbols from gravestones, like this 18th-century examole from Scotland

THE JOLLY ROGER, a flag emblazoned with emblems of death, warned pirates' victims to surrender without a fight. Although the Jolly Roger filled mariners with dread, it was less feared than a plain red flag, which signaled death to all who saw it and meant the pirates would show no mercy in the ensuing battle. But the threatening Jolly Roger usually served its purpose. Some crews defended their ships bravely, but often sailors were keen to surrender, sometimes opting to join the pirates. Worked to death and close to mutiny anyway, many sailors saw piracy as a life of freedom and wealth, with only a slim chance of being caught.

A LEGEND IN THE MAKING
The flag of Henry Avery (p. 47) closely resembles the skull-and-crossbones Jolly Roger of pirate legend. In the 1600s, the skull and crossbones was commonly used to represent death, and it was adopted by pirates toward the end of the century. However, the skull and crossbones was not a standard pirate emblem; every pirate had his own particular Jolly Roger design.

A SCIMITAR TOO FAR
The sword has always been a symbol of power, so the message of Thomas Tew's (p. 47) flag was plain to all. However, the choice of the curved Asian scimitar was an unfortunate one for Tew, for it may have been a similar sword that slew him in the battle for the Indian ship *Futteh Mahmood* in 1695.

TIME FLIES
The hourglass appears on many pirate flags. On English pirate Christopher Moody's (1694-1722) flag, as on many gravestones of the age, the glass had wings to show how rapidly the sand was running out. A traditional symbol of death, the hourglass warned sailors that the time for surrender was limited.

Not all pirate flags were black and white

Pirates pretending to be female passengers to deceive an approaching ship

MASTERS OF DECEPTION
Pirates would have probably fared poorly in a conventional naval battle, so they often relied on deception and terror to trap their prey. When approaching a target, pirates sometimes flew a friendly flag, then at the last minute raised a Jolly Roger to terrify their victims into surrendering without a fight. If this failed, they launched a surprise attack, boarded the ship, and overpowered the crew.

A PIRATE SEAMSTRESS
Jolly Rogers were rough-and-ready affairs, run up by a pirate ship's sailmaker or any other member of the crew. Pirates of New Providence Island in the Bahamas had flags made for them by a sailmaker's widow who accepted payment in brandy.

THE FLAG WAS BOLD
Women pirates Mary Read and Anne Bonny (pp. 32–33) probably fought under this emblem of a skull and crossed swords. It was the flag flown by their pirate captain Jack Rackham (p. 32). However, Rackham wasn't as bold as his flag suggested. When the British navy attacked his ship, he hid in the hold with the rest of his drunken men, leaving the two women to fight alone.

BLOODY BLACKBEARD
Blackbeard's (pp. 30–31) flag shows a devil-like skeleton holding an hourglass, an arrow, and a bleeding heart. The Jolly Roger may have been named after the devil – Old Roger – but it probably got its name from the French term for the red flag – *Jolie Rouge*.

FORTUNE FAVORS THE FAST
Pirate ships and those of their victims varied widely, so there was no single method of attack. However, pirates usually had no trouble overtaking their quarry, because they generally used small, fast ships; the merchant ships they preyed upon were more heavily built and slowed by heavy cargo.

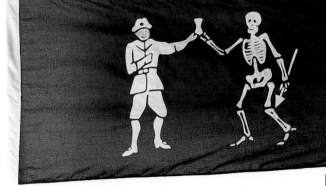

DRINKING WITH DEATH
Drinking with a skeleton, Bartholomew Roberts (p. 39) toasted death on his flag. He also flew a second flag that showed him astride two skulls, labeled ABH and AMH. The initials stood for "A Barbadian's Head" and "A Martinican's Head" – a vow of revenge against two Caribbean islands that dared cross him.

Pirate treasure

WHEN PIRATES SWARMED ABOARD a heavily laden ship, they hoped to find a hold full of gold. If they were lucky, the prize could make the entire crew wealthy beyond their wildest dreams. When Thomas Tew (p. 47) raided a ship in the Indian Ocean in 1693, every member of the ship's crew received a share then worth £3,000 (British pounds) – a sum equal today to over $3.5 million! But such massive prizes were exceptional. More often, the pirate crews divided up much more modest treasures or, worse, discovered a hold full of a bulky cargo.

Rose-sapphire cross pendant

SWAGGER DAGGER
When the cargo was not worth plundering, pirates contented themselves with robbing passengers and stealing their valuables. An elaborate dagger like this one was too good for fighting, but it would fetch a fine price.

Piece of eight

X MARKS THE SPOT
Buried hoards of pirate treasure are mostly romantic myths, although William Kidd (p. 46), right, did bury treasure at Gardiners Island, just off the eastern tip of Long Island, New York. It was all recovered.

Emerald salamander

SPANISH GOLD
A pirate's favorite booty was Spanish gold or silver. A Spanish gold doubloon was worth about seven weeks' pay for an ordinary sailor. Silver pieces of eight, or old Spanish pesos, could be cut into pieces to make small change.

Gold doubloon

Bloodstone reliquary

Garnet fan holder

Rose sapphire

Malachite

Rose-sapphire cross

Pirates would have forced the lid of this multiple-lock strongbox

Late 16th-century English money chest

Gold seal ring

Ruby

Garnet

Amethyst

Large ruby

Enameled cross

JEWELS TO DIE FOR
Dividing a cargo of precious gems fairly wasn't always easy. One raid on a Portuguese East Indiaman in 1721 rewarded each of the crew with £4,000 ($4.3 million today) and 42 small diamonds. One crewman was given one large diamond instead of 42 little ones; unhappy with his share, he broke it into smaller pieces with a hammer!

SHARING OUT THE SPOILS
Pirates divided up a haul more or less equally, although the captain and other "officers" usually received more than others. The carpenter sometimes got less, because he did not risk his life in the attacks. Under one typical scheme, the captain received 2.5 times as much as a seaman, the surgeon 1.25 times, but the carpenter got just three quarters of a share. Boys got a half share.

WELL WORTH ITS WEIGHT
At right, Henry Avery (p. 47) and his crew load heavy treasure chests from the captured Arab ship *Gang-i-Sawai*. This haul was reputed to be the equivalent of around £325,000 (over $400 million today). Each crew member received around £2,000 ($2.5 million today), and Avery himself was able to retire from piracy on the proceeds.

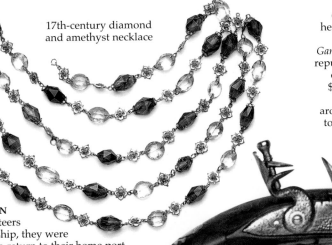

17th-century diamond and amethyst necklace

PRIZE POSSESSION
After privateers boarded a ship, they were supposed to return to their home port before dividing the cargo. However, the crew were often entitled to pillage, or steal the personal possessions of passengers and crew, such as this expensive necklace.

Tiger's eye

Sapphire

Ruby

Rubies

PRECIOUS PISTOL
Weapons and ammunition were highly prized booty among pirates.

TEMPTING TRINKETS
Privateers were supposed to divvy up pillaged goods according to rank, but, in practice, many just pocketed small items such as these gold rings.

LIFESAVING LOOT
Pirates often relied on stealing everyday necessities from their victims. Food and medicine were usually in short supply. One victim of pirates in 1720 reported, "No part of the cargo was so much valued by the robbers as the doctor's chest, for they were all poxed to a great degree."

18th-century ship's medicine chest

SNUFF SAID
The taking of snuff, which was finely ground tobacco, became fashionable around 1680, at the height of buccaneer activity on the Spanish Main. A ship's wealthy passengers often carried elaborately decorated snuffboxes that made attractive trinkets for plunderers.

Dutch snuffbox made of copper alloy

Garnet

Opal

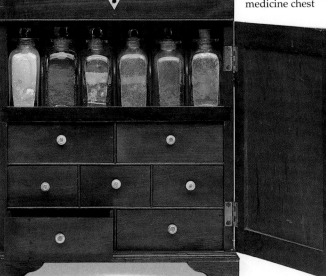

Piracy and slavery

WHEN PIRATES CAPTURED a merchant ship, they often found a cargo of human misery. In the dark hold were hundreds of African slaves bound for the American colonies. The slave trade was big business in the 17th and 18th centuries, with slaves sold in the Americas for 10 to 15 times their cost in Africa. These huge profits lured the pirates. Some became slavers and others sold cargoes of slaves captured at sea. Many slipped easily between the occupations of slaver, privateer, and pirate – by the 1830s the term "picaroon" had come to mean both "pirate" and "slaver." But the end of the slave trade was in sight. After 1815, the British Royal Navy stopped slave ships from crossing the Atlantic, and the slave trade soon died out.

CRUEL YOKE
This barbarous iron collar was designed to keep a slave from escaping through the bush. Savage punishments for recaptured runaways discouraged slaves from attempting escape.

Heavy chain

DISHONORABLE CAREER
John Hawkins (1532–95) was the first English privateer to realize that the slave trade was big business. In 1562, he made the first of three voyages as a slaver, sailing from England to West Africa, where he loaded 300 slaves. Hawkins then sailed to the Caribbean and sold his human cargo on the island of Hispaniola.

BUYING SLAVES
European slave traders bought slaves from African chiefs with cheap goods or manillas – bars of iron, brass, and copper that were used as money in West Africa.

Manillas

Britain
America
Caribbean
Atlantic
Jamaica
Africa
The middle passage

THE SLAVE TRADE TRIANGLE
Slave ships sailed from England or America with cargoes of cheap goods. In Africa, these were exchanged for slaves, and the ships sailed on to the Caribbean – this leg of the voyage was called the "middle passage." On islands like Jamaica, the slaves were exchanged for sugar, molasses, or hardwoods before the ships sailed home. A profit was made at every stage.

Diagram showing the cramped, inhumane conditions inside a slave ship hold

SLAVE REVOLT
Outnumbered by their cargo of slaves, the crew members of a slave ship lived in constant fear of revolt. Rebellions were savagely repressed, although there was little chance of escaping from a slave ship. The odds for runaway slaves were greater if they managed to escape from a plantation.

Long bar sticks out from the neck

DEATH SHIP
Many slaves died during the middle passage, so slavers packed as many slaves as possible into the holds. There was no sanitation, and disease spread rapidly – the dead often lay alongside the living for days.

Hook designed to catch on undergrowth to prevent a fast escape through the bush

GANG CHAIN
Rebellious slaves were chained together and made to work in a "chain gang."

Neck collar

WORKED TO DEATH
Cutting sugarcane in tropical heat was backbreaking work. African slaves were used because this job was considered too hard for Europeans. However, many slaves were literally worked to death on the sugar plantations.

AN INFAMOUS PIRATE SLAVER
Pirates often raided African slave ports. This engraving shows English pirate Bartholomew Roberts (1682–1722) at Whydah (present-day Ouidah, Benin), where he captured 11 slave ships. Roberts began his career in 1719, loading slaves at an African trading post. Pirates attacked the post and carried Roberts away; he soon became their leader.

Several slaves were chained to one bar

Iron bar was nailed to the floor of the ship's hold

Heavy iron neck collar was extremely uncomfortable to wear

ANKLE FETTERS
On board ship, slaves were kept in ankle fetters to prevent them from rebelling or committing suicide to escape the horror of the stinking hold. This also meant the slaves were unable to defend themselves against pirates.

Fetter fit around the ankle

NEW LIFE AS A PIRATE
The connection between slavery and piracy wasn't entirely one-sided. Pirate captains in the Caribbean welcomed runaway slaves, who made up as much as a third of some pirate crews. Joining a pirate ship must have seemed an attractive choice compared to the appalling sufferings of a slave's life.

THE COST OF SUGAR
This painting shows a highly idealized view of life on an Antiguan sugar plantation. The reality was very different. Slaves worked 10 hours a day, six days a week. Those who fell asleep on the job could lose limbs in crushing machines or tumble into vats of boiling syrup. Pirates added to the risks, sometimes raiding coastal plantations to steal slaves for resale.

Leather lash

Handle reinforced with stitching

Whip suspended by loop formed slaver's belt

HARSH TREATMENT
Slaves who fled their plantations to join pirate ships escaped from a world of horrible cruelty. The whip was the standard punishment for the most trivial crimes, and flogging crippled many slaves.

Life at sea

LIFE ON A PIRATE SHIP was full of contrast. Seizing a prize meant moments of great excitement and terrifying danger. But in between there might be weeks of mind-numbing tedium. No wonder pirate crews quarreled! To control a crew's boredom and frustration, a "captain" had to command respect – or fear – for many pirates ran their ships as democratic communities. If they couldn't agree on a course, they took a vote. Even the captain's job wasn't secure. If the crew disagreed with him, they held an election – this is how Bartholomew Sharp (p. 24) came to command a pirate cruise in 1680.

CAT-O'-NINE-TAILS
The traditional maritime whip was the cat-o'-nine-tails. The sailor to be whipped made it himself by unwinding a rope into its three strands, then further unwinding and knotting each strand. Each "cat" was used only once – if used repeatedly, its bloody cords would infect the wounds it inflicted.

Knotted end tore the flesh

UP ALOFT
On pirate ships, muscles did all the work. The crew had to pull together to keep the ship moving, and keeping up speed meant constant adjustments to the sails and rigging.

Curved needles for sewing wounds

Canvas case rolled up to fit in pocket

Spoon to remove shot from wound

Waxed cotton thread

Sharp knife for making rapid incisions

Late-18th-century surgeon's kit

MAKE DO AND MEND
Repairs filled many of the long hours at sea; the sails, for instance, needed constant patching where they flapped against the masts and ropes. To protect their hands as they forced needles through the tough hemp sails, pirates used a leather "palm."

Reinforced area holds the needle end

Thumb hole

MEND OR STEAL?
All seamen could splice and join ropes, but pirates preferred to steal replacements. When Bartholomew Roberts (p. 31) captured the *King Solomon*, his crew stole ropes and sails, but threw her cargo overboard.

UNDER THE KNIFE
Though pirates valued the services of a physician, there was little one could do for serious injuries except sew up the wound. Surgery almost always led to fatal infection and death. A surgeon carried a kit like this and would also use a saw to remove shattered limbs.

GETTING TO KNOW THE ROPES
After a storm or battle, a crew labored to mend ropes and sails on a shattered ship. Basil Ringrose (p. 26) describes how, in 1679: "We took out of [a Spanish prize] some osnaburgs (coarse linen) of which we made top-gallant sails."

Pirate riggers used a wooden fid or metal marlinespike to separate strands of rope for splicing

Splicing joined rope or made endings that would not unwind

Clean cords suggest that this "cat" was never used

Pirate contract

Some pirate crews had a code of conduct that all agreed to obey. These rules, from Charles Johnson's 18th-century book on pirates (p. 61), are typical:

I. Every man has a vote in affairs of the moment; has equal title to the fresh provisions or strong liquors.
II. No person to game at cards or dice for money.
III. The lights and candles to be put out at eight o'clock at night.
IV. To keep their piece [musket], pistols, and cutlass clean and fit for service.
V. No boy or woman to be allowed amongst them.
VI. To desert the ship in battle was punished with death or marooning.

Fabric covers rope to make handle

A FLOGGING
When pirates captured a vessel, they treated officers much as officers had in turn treated their crews. Captains who had imposed severe discipline, with floggings for minor offenses, might get a taste of their own medicine on the pirate ship.

Yardarm

Swivel guns were quick to aim and load but had short range

British flag (red ensign) was one of many the ship carried

Captain and a few other "officers" had cabins at stern

Barrels of drinking water (or rocks and gravel) helped balance ship

Space below deck was cramped, because ships carried enough pirates to crew prize ships

PIRATE FLAGSHIP
Pirate ships varied widely. Small, fast sloops were ideal for inshore raiding, but much bigger vessels, such as this three-masted square-rigger, were safer on the open ocean. The size of the ship alone was enough to scare the wits out of many of the pirates' intended victims. This drawing is based on the *Whydah* (one of the few known wrecks of a pirate ship) which sank off the coast of Wellfleet, Massachusetts, in 1717.

FURRY FIEND
Every pirate ship had a population of rats. They were more than just a nuisance, for they devoured food and could even gnaw their way right through the hull, sinking the vessel.

Food on board

"NOT BOILED TURTLE AGAIN?!" For hungry pirates the menu was short: when there was fresh meat, it was usually turtle. When turtles couldn't be found and the fish didn't bite, the pirates survived on biscuits or dried meat washed down with beer or wine. Monotony, however, was better than the starvation that pirates faced when shipwrecked or becalmed. Then, they might be reduced to eating their satchels or even each other. When food ran out on Charlotte de Berry's (p. 33) ship, the crew reputedly ate two slaves and then devoured her husband!

TASTY TUNA
In the Caribbean, pirates could catch fish fairly easily. In his buccaneering journal, Basil Ringrose recorded, "The sea hereabouts is very full of several sorts of fish, as dolphins, bonitos, albicores, mullets and old wives, etc. which came swimming about our ship in whole shoals."

A CLUBBED SANDWICH
Pirates lived off the land wherever they could. On remote islands, animals and birds were unused to being hunted and were often quite tame. The pirates could catch them with their bare hands.

16th-century mariners clubbing tame turtle doves

PROVISIONING A SHIP
Even far from a port, a carefully chosen island could supply pirates with all the provisions they needed. These buccaneers are shown restocking their ship with fresh meat, water, and timber. In his journal of buccaneer life (p. 26), Ringrose recounts, "Having made this island, we resolved to go thither and refit our rigging and get some goats which there run wild."

POACHED POUCH
In 1670, Henry Morgan's (p. 27) band of half-starved buccaneers were so hungry that they resorted to eating their satchels! One of them left the recipe: "Slice the leather into pieces, then soak and beat and rub between stones to tenderise. Scrape off the hair, and roast or grill. Cut into smaller pieces and serve with lots of water."

TURTLE HUNTERS
Captain Johnson (p. 61) recounts, "The manner of catching [turtles] is very particular...As soon as they land, the men...turn them on their backs...and leave them until morning, where they are sure to find them, for they can't turn again, nor move from that place."

Heavy shell makes the turtle slow on land

Large flippers for swimming

PIRATE PREY
Sea turtles were plentiful throughout the Caribbean and provided one of the few sources of fresh meat available to pirates. Agile in the sea, turtles were slow on land and easy prey for foraging pirates. On board ship, the cook could keep turtles alive in the hold until it was time to cook them. Soft-shelled turtle eggs were also a popular pirate delicacy.

FRESH EGGS

Like other ships of the 17th and 18th centuries, pirate vessels would have carried hens to provide fresh eggs and meat. The nautical nickname for eggs was "cackle-fruit," for the distinctive noise a hen makes when laying.

Hard-baked biscuit made of flour and water

HARDTACK

Long-lasting ship's biscuits were a staple food for most mariners. They were known as hardtack because they were so tough. On board a ship, biscuits soon became infested with weevils, so pirates preferred to eat them in the dark!

PREVENTIVE MEDICINE

On long voyages, poor diets meant that pirates suffered from diseases such as scurvy, which is caused by a lack of vitamin C. However, in 1753, it was discovered that eating fresh fruit, particularly limes, could prevent scurvy.

Bottle for wine or brandy – favorite pirate drinks

Hen's egg, a good source of protein

SERVED ON A PLATE

Pirates ate from pewter plates like this one, but they were not well known for their table manners. Describing ravenous buccaneers, Exquemeling (p. 62) wrote, "Such was their hunger that they more resembled cannibals than Europeans..., the blood many times running down from their beards."

Expensive knife would have been pillaged from another ship

Fork folds into its handle, making it easy to carry in a pocket or pouch

Plate made of pewter, an alloy of tin and lead

A BOTTLE OF BEER

Without any method of preservation, water on board ship quickly became undrinkable, and all mariners preferred beer or wine. Even naval vessels carried huge quantities of beer, though usually in barrels rather than bottles.

Without an opener, pirates just struck off the bottle's neck with a cutlass

COOKING IN CALM SEAS

Captain Kidd's (p. 46) ship, *The Adventure Galley*, below, had no kitchen quarters, only a caldron that was too dangerous to use in rough weather.

KNIFE AND FORK ETIQUETTE

Although forks were sometimes used, crude pirates probably ate only with knives and spoons, or with their fingers.

Earthenware beer bottle, 17th century

A JUG OF WINE

Washed down with a half gallon of plundered wine from a pewter tankard, almost any food became just about tolerable.

Life on land

CRAMMED TOGETHER FOR MONTHS in a stinking, often unseaworthy ship, pirates and buccaneers had plenty of time to dream about life on land. When they reached a port, many were wealthy enough to buy practically anything they'd dreamed of. They squandered their booty on drinking, women, and gambling. One eyewitness recalled: "Such of these pirates are found who will spend two or three thousand pieces-of-eight in one night, not leaving themselves a good shirt of their backs." Two pieces-of-eight bought a cow, so the pirates gambled away the equivalent of a whole farm. But life on land wasn't always one long party. In between wild drinking bouts and gambling sessions, there was always work to be done. The crew had to careen, or beach and repair, their ship, and take on board fresh water and provisions for the next villainous voyage.

MONEY CAN BUY YOU LOVE
Women were banned from most pirate ships, but they often came on board when the ships were moored in harbor. After a long voyage, pirates usually went in search of female company. There were many women in Caribbean ports who were glad to share in the pirates' booty and join in their wild carousing.

Heavy handle swung with both hands

Pirates rest and careen their ship

CAREENED AND CLEANED
Seaweed and barnacles grew rapidly on the bottoms of ships, greatly reducing their speed. Worse, worms bored tiny holes that could eventually sink a ship. Pirate crews solved the problem by regular careening.

Mallet for striking the irons

Ramming iron

Caulking mallet

Jerry iron

Caulking iron

Pitch ladle

Broad blade for splitting open rotten seams

Narrow blade for driving in new oakum

Angled blade for hacking old oakum from seams

Adz

Strong, chisel-like blade for chipping off barnacles and seaweed

TOOLS OF THE TRADE
Wooden ships required regular maintenance if they were to remain seaworthy. Pirate crews had tools like these to carry out essential jobs. Caulking, which involved repairing the seams between planks, was vital to keep the ship watertight. The seams were stripped, filled with oakum, or unraveled rope, and sealed with hot pitch.

Funnel-like tip for pouring hot pitch into seams

BLACK JACK

Pirates were welcome in dockside taverns. There, pirates washed the salt from their throats with copious quantities of beer and wine, probably served in black jacks – leather tankards made watertight and rigid with a coating of pitch.

Silver rim

MIDNIGHT REVELLING

In this picture, the crews of Blackbeard (pp. 30–31) and Charles Vane are carousing the night away on Ocracoke Island off the North Carolina coast. Not all ports welcomed pirates, and crews often holed up in a favorite pirate hideaway to celebrate a successful raid.

17th-century playing cards commemorating a famous political plot

A HAND OF CARDS

Gambling for money was forbidden on board many pirate ships, probably because it caused fights. On shore, pirate crews could soon be parted from their share of a prize by a crooked card game.

Wooden dice

SPENDING SPREES

Pirates were welcome in many ports, since crews were famous for spending money with wild abandon.

BUCCANEER BASE

Port Royal in Jamaica, above, was a magnet for 17th-century pirates seeking pleasure ashore. British governors welcomed the pirates, believing their presence would protect the island from Spanish attacks. In 1692, Port Royal was destroyed by an earthquake, which many believed was divine judgment on this corrupt town.

A PEACEFUL PIPE

A pipeful of tobacco was an onshore luxury for pirates. Wooden ships caught fire easily, so crews chewed tobacco at sea rather than risk smoking.

Clay pipestem has snapped off

Lid to keep out flies

TANKARD UP

Glass was costly and fragile, so the keepers of many taverns greeted pirates with brimming pewter tankards. These were strong enough to withstand a night of revelry.

YO HO HO AND A BOTTLE OF RUM

The reputation of pirates as rum-swilling bandits was largely true. They drank anything alcoholic, and many were never sober while onshore. One notorious drunk would buy a huge barrel of wine and place it in the street. He would force everyone who passed by to drink with him, threatening them with a pistol.

17th-century liquor bottles

OLD CALABAR CAREENAGE

A secluded beach was essential for careening because pirates were defenseless during the work. Old Calabar River on the Guinea coast of Africa was an ideal spot because it was too shallow for most ships to pursue the pirates' small crafts. In the picture above, Bartholomew Roberts's (p. 39) crew relaxes by the river after a hard day's caulking.

Pirates of the Indian Ocean

An East Indiaman

WHEN THE RICH PICKINGS on the Spanish Main (p. 20) declined, many pirates sailed east to the Indian Ocean. They were lured by the treasure fleets of the Indian Moghul Empire and the great merchantmen of the British, French, and Dutch East India Companies. Most of the pirates made for Madagascar off the east coast of Africa. This wild island was ideally placed for raiding European trade routes to India and Muslim pilgrimage routes to the Red Sea. The pirates soon amassed large fortunes, and the likes of Kidd and Avery acquired legendary status. But their activities damaged trade and aroused anti-European feeling in India, causing governments to act against the pirates.

William Kidd buries his Bible in a mythical episode from his life

CAPTAIN KIDD
Scottish-born William Kidd (c.1645–1701) was a New York businessman sent to the Indian Ocean to hunt Avery and his colleagues. However, under pressure from his ruffian crew, Kidd committed several acts of piracy himself. On his return, Kidd was tried and hanged as a pirate.

Mecca

Avery captured the Gang-i-Sawai *near the Indus River*

Red Sea · India · China · Surat · Africa · Sumatra · Indian Ocean · Java · Madagascar

Cape of Good Hope

GOOD HOPE FOR PIRATES
After rounding the Cape of Good Hope, European trade ships took one of two different courses on their way to India and China. But both routes passed within a few hundred miles of Madagascar, the pirates' island lair.

Ratlines hanging from the rigging enabled sailors to climb above the deck; once aloft, they were better able to fight off an attack from a pirate ship

GLITTERING PRIZES
Indian ships seized by pirates yielded rich hauls of gems. One of Avery's crew who raided the *Gang-i-Sawai* recalled, "We took great quantities of jewels and a saddle and bridle set with rubies."

EAST INDIAMEN
Laden with luxury goods, East Indiamen were the favorite prey of pirates. These great merchant ships traded between Europe and Asia in the 17th and 18th centuries. On the journey to Asia, the East Indiamen were loaded with gold and silver; they carried fine china, silks, and exotic spices to Europe from the East.

PIRATE PARADISE
The tropical island paradise of Madagascar acquired an exotic reputation. Popular legends told how the pirates there lived like princes. According to 18th-century writer Captain Johnson, "They married the most beautiful of the negro women, not one or two but as many as they liked."

A BRILLIANT CAREER
The English pirate Henry Avery (1665–c.1728) became notorious for his capture of the Moghul's ship *Gang-i-Sawai*, which was carrying pilgrims and treasure from Surat to Mecca. The brutal treatment of the passengers aroused a furious response from the Moghul, who demanded retribution from the British authorities.

PRICELESS PORCELAIN
Fine Chinese porcelain was highly prized in 17th- and 18th-century Europe. After 1684, when the Chinese allowed the British East India Company to open a trading station at Canton, the East Indiamen carried tons of "china" across the Indian Ocean.

St. Mary's Island

HIGH-SOCIETY PIRATE
American-born Thomas Tew led what became known as "the pirate round," sailing from North America to the Indian Ocean and returning with booty. At home he was a celebrity and is seen here relating his adventures to his friend the governor of New York. Tew was killed on an expedition with Avery in 1695.

During battles, sailors stood on the maintop to fire at the pirate ships

SAFE HAVEN
More like a small continent than an island, Madagascar was an ideal hideout for the pirates of the Indian Ocean. In the late 17th century, this wild, tropical island was uncolonized by Europeans and therefore safe for outlaws. All the same, the ever-wary pirates created a fortified base at St. Mary's Island on Madagascar's northeast coast that could easily be defended if necessary.

East Indiaman is heavily armed to resist attack by pirates

Tea leaves

Green coffee beans

Pepper

Cloves

SURPLUS SPICE
Pirates who captured a cargo of spices from an East Indiaman often dumped their haul, because spices were bulky and difficult to sell. In 1720, a Madagascar beach was reported to be a foot deep in pepper and cloves.

Large hold for carrying bulky cargoes and provisions for many weeks made the ship slow and cumbersome

Nutmegs

Cinnamon sticks

COSTLY CUP
Cargoes of tea and coffee could fetch a big profit in Europe (in 1700, a pound of tea cost more than two weeks' wages for a laborer) but pirates preferred to capture wine or brandy! But one pirate, Bartholomew Roberts (p. 39), preferred tea to alcohol; he thought drunkenness impaired a ship's efficiency.

Desert islands

MAROONED ALONE ON AN ISLAND, a disgraced pirate watched helplessly as his ship sailed away. A desert island was a prison without walls. The sea prevented escape, and the chances of being rescued were slim. Although marooned pirates were left with a few essential provisions, starvation faced those who could not hunt and fish. This cruel punishment was meted out to pirates who stole from their comrades or deserted their ship in battle. When leaky pirate ships ran aground, survivors of the wrecks faced the same lonely fate.

THE CASTAWAY
Shipwrecked pirates endured the same sense of isolation as those marooned for a crime. Their only hope of rescue was to watch for a sail on the horizon.

BARE NECESSITIES
A marooned pirate was put ashore with only meager supplies. English captain John Phillips's pirate code stated that the victim should be given "one bottle of Powder, one bottle of water, one small arm, and shot." But the unlucky man usually had no way of cooking or keeping warm. One kind pirate secretly gave a marooned man "a tinder box with materials in it for striking fire; which, in his circumstances, was a greater present than gold or jewels."

DEFENSE
A pistol was fine for defense against animals; a musket was better for hunting.

A DAY'S GRACE
A small bottle of water lasted just a day or so. After that, the castaway had to find water on his own.

ALEXANDER SELKIRK
Sick of arguments on his ship, Scottish privateer Alexander Selkirk (1676–1721) actually asked to be marooned. By the time he'd changed his mind, the ship had sailed away. To amuse himself, the castaway tamed wild cats and goats and taught them to dance.

THE FORGOTTEN ISLE
Alexander Selkirk's home from 1704 to 1709 was Más á Tierra (present-day Robinson Crusoe) an island in the South Pacific 400 mi (640 km) west of Chile. One of the Juan Fernández Islands, it had a good supply of water and teemed with wild pigs and goats. Selkirk lived largely on goat meat and palm cabbage and dressed in goatskins. When he was found by his rescuers, he was ragged and dirty, but did not want to leave his island home.

ROBINSON CRUSOE
This most famous of all fictional castaways was the creation of English author Daniel Defoe (1660–1731). He based the story on the life of Alexander Selkirk, but gave Crusoe a "savage" companion, Friday. Crusoe spent more than a quarter of a century on his island and lived more comfortably than any real castaway: "In this plentiful manner, I lived; neither could I be said to want anything but society."

A LONELY FATE
In this imaginative painting by American illustrator Howard Pyle (1853–1911), a lonely pirate awaits death on the beach of a desert island. In fact, marooned pirates didn't have time to brood on their fate. Most who survived stressed how busy they were finding food.

Gunpowder

Musket balls

Powder horn

SHIPWRECKED
Pirates often took over a captured vessel, but if the ship was unseaworthy, they could easily find themselves shipwrecked on a deserted shore. The same fate befell pirate crews who became drunk, which was fairly common, and neglected navigation.

KINDNESS DOESN'T PAY
English pirate Edward England (died 1720) fell out with his crew while sailing off the coast of Africa. Accused of being too kind to a prisoner, England and two others were marooned by their merciless comrades on the island of Mauritius. According to one account, the three escaped by building a boat and sailing to Madagascar, where England died soon after.

IN SHORT SUPPLY
The gunpowder stored in this powder horn would soon run out, and after that castaways had to be ingenious. One group of pirates marooned in the Bahamas lived by "feeding upon berries and shellfish [and] sometimes catching a stingray… by the help of a sharpened stick."

The French corsairs

THE FRENCH KNEW ST. MALO as La Cité Corsaire, but to the English, it was a "nest of wasps." By any name, the French port of St. Malo in the 17th century was a town grown rich on the profits of privateering. For many local people, privateering, or *la course*, was a family trade, one in which son followed father to sea. The French corsairs emerged in the 9th century when the merchant ships of Brittany armed themselves against the marauding Vikings. When the Viking threat ended during the 11th century, there was no shortage of targets, for France was frequently at war. England was most often the victim of the wasps' stings, and in 1693, the English built a disguised bomb ship to destroy the nest. However, their floating bomb exploded noisily in St. Malo harbor with just one French casualty – a cat. The English fleet sailed away humiliated, and the corsairs continued well into the next century.

PISTOLS OF A PRIVATEER
Robert Surcouf was famous not only for his brilliance as a corsair but also for his personal bravery. His handsome pistols were not just decoration – Surcouf once took on a dozen Prussian soldiers in a fight and won.

Scratches indicate the pistol was well used

Pistol butt cap in the shape of an eagle

Marble statue of Réné Duguay-Trouin, one of St. Malo's most famous sons

Surcouf's own pair of flintlock pistols

Surcouf's name (just visible) is engraved on the trigger guard

HEROES OF THE HIGH SEAS

Renowned for their daring deeds, the French corsairs were national heroes. They were famous because they were patriots fighting for France, but also because privateering was profitable. Many Brittany families grew rich on the proceeds, and even the Bishop of St Malo invested in *la course*. Ships and streets were named after the corsairs: this romantic ship's figurehead portrays Duguay-Trouin.

17th-century
ship's figurehead

DUNKIRK
The hometown of Jean Bart, Dunkirk (in northern France) was hot property while he was a boy: it was by turns Spanish, French, and English territory. Finally in French hands, the port became a corsair base to rival St. Malo.

JEAN BART
Jean Bart (1651–1702) preyed upon ships in the English Channel and the North Sea. Famed for his daring, after being captured by the English, he escaped to France by rowing 150 miles in a small boat.

ROBERT SURCOUF
Born a century after Duguay-Trouin, Robert Surcouf (1773–1827), left, practiced the corsair trade far from his St. Malo home. His base was the French-owned island of Mauritius in the Indian Ocean. From there he raided British merchant ships heading for Indian ports.

Brass
barrel

Ramrod

CAPTURING *THE KENT*
Surcouf's most heroic feat was to capture the British East Indiaman *Kent*. This painting shows Surcouf's men boarding the huge 38-gun merchant ship from their much smaller ship, the *Confiance*. One of the captured crew sneered that the French fought only for profit, whereas the English fought for honor, to which Surcouf replied, "That only proves that each of us fights to acquire something he does not possess."

Missiles

Incendiary
bombs

Barrels of
explosives

AN INFERNAL DISASTER
This infernal machine, right, was sent against the Malouins by the English as a lethal weapon. Packed full of explosives, this 85-ft- (26-m-) long bomb ship sat high in the water so that it could sail close to St. Malo's city wall. But on the night of the attack, the ship hit a rock, seawater moistened the gunpowder, and the bomb went off like a damp firecracker.

Barrels of
gunpowder

THE CORSAIR CAPITAL
The corsair promoters, or *armateurs*, of the island St. Malo flourished. By the 18th century, when this view was drawn, they had become so wealthy that even the French king borrowed money from them to pay for his wars.

American privateers

THE AMERICAN REVOLUTION (1775–83) showed off privateer power as few wars had done before. The tiny Continental (American) navy fought the British with just 34 ships. But more than 400 privateer ships attacked British merchant shipping, crippling trade. One 18th-century English writer complained, "All commerce with America is at an end...survey our docks; count there the gallant ships laid up and useless." As in previous wars, those who lost ships to privateers dismissed them as "pirates." The English victims used the word loosely, including even Continental navy officers, such as John Paul Jones. After independence, the U.S. needed to boost its naval strength with privateers just once more, when war with Britain broke out in 1812. But the speedy ships were never again as effective as in the days when they helped secure their nation's freedom.

DASHING NAVAL HERO
Dashing raids on the coastal lands of Britain perhaps earned John Paul Jones the label of "pirate," but his actions at sea were what made him well known at home. In his most famous battle, he maneuvered his vessel alongside a British warship and lashed the two together. British guns almost sank his ship, but Jones dismissed calls to surrender with the words: "I have not yet begun to fight!" Three hours later, the British gave in.

AFRICAN PRIZES
An Englishman writing from Grenada in 1777 complained bitterly that the American privateers had captured "some thousand weight of gold dust."

HUMBLE CARGOES
Ships captured by privateers did not always contain costly luxuries. Ordinary foods such as salt and rice fed Revolutionary American troops – and their loss starved the British foe.

Rice

Salt

ELEPHANT TEETH
American-bound exports lost to privateers in the Revolutionary War included a cargo of ivory. Insurance costs rose sixfold for ships sailing without protection.

UNARMED COMBAT
The largest colonial American port, Philadelphia equipped many plucky privateers. One of them, the brig *Despatch*, sailed unarmed from this port in 1776, hoping to capture guns from a British ship in the Atlantic! Amazingly, the crew succeeded within a few days and sailed on to France.

PATRIOT'S BUST

Neither pirate nor privateer, John Paul Jones (1747–92) was in some ways a bit of both. Apprenticed on a merchant ship then mate on a slaver, he fled the Caribbean to escape a murder charge. His career in the Continental navy began in 1775, and Jones's daring deeds over the next six years made him a national hero. Political rivalry later in life left him bitter and broken, and he died in 1792.

BLUFFING PRIVATEER

Jonathan Haraden (1745–1803) once sailed alongside an English ship, hoisted the bloody flag, and demanded surrender in five minutes. Then he stood watch with a lighted wick by a cannon and waited. The ship surrendered, but Haraden was bluffing – the cannon was loaded with his only remaining shot.

TOPSAIL SCHOONER

American privateers who used specially built ships favored topsail schooners like the vessel shown here outside New Orleans harbor. These very fast, fairly small ships had two masts, the foremast shorter than the mainmast. Rigging a square sail at the top of the foremast boosted speed with a tail wind.

PRIVATEER CITY

With a natural harbor in Chesapeake Bay, Baltimore was a traditional shipbuilding center. Some of the first privateering vessels of the Revolutionary War – at first converted merchant ships, but later expressly built schooners – sailed from this Maryland city.

JEAN LAFITTE

Haitian-born pirate, privateer, slaver, and smuggler, Jean Lafitte (c. 1780–c. 1826) and his brother Pierre ran an underworld gang that provided about one-tenth of the jobs in New Orleans around 1807. Outlawed for smuggling slaves, Lafitte earned a pardon by defending the city against attack in the War of 1812.

GULF ATTACK

The Lafittes' pirate attacks were mainly on Spanish vessels in the Gulf of Mexico. They claimed that these raids were legitimate privateering and held letters of marque to prove it. But they also took American prizes and secretly traded slaves through their stronghold at Barataria Bay near New Orleans.

Pirates of the China Sea

Three masts with four-sided sails of bamboo matting

Captain and his family had quarters at the stern of the ship. Crew lived in the cramped hold

THE SEAS AND CHANNELS OF CHINA and Southeast Asia were a pirate's paradise. Small boats could hide easily in the mangrove swamps along the coasts. Pirates were exploiting this characteristic by A.D. 400, combining sea robbery with local warfare. China and Japan often had to act together to suppress them. When Europeans set up empires in the 16th and 17th centuries, the situation worsened. The early-17th-century pirate Ching-Chi-ling led a fleet of 1,000 heavily armed vessels, together with many slaves and bodyguards. The Europeans acted against these powerful pirates and by the 1860s had stamped them out.

BARBER PIRATE
Hong Kong barber Chui Apoo (died 1851) joined the fleet of pirate chief Shap'n'gtzai (active in the 1840s) in 1845 and was soon appointed his lieutenant.

THE END OF THE ROAD
British navy gunboats destroyed Chui Apoo's fleet in 1849 as part of a campaign against pirate chief Shap'n'gtzai.

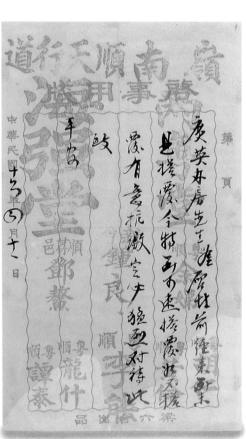

Strait of Malacca was a hunting ground for pirates

Mouth of Canton River was pirate center from the 1760s

China

South China Sea

Sumatra

Borneo

Java

THE SEAS OF SOUTHEAST ASIA
Though large fleets sometimes dominated piracy in eastern Asia, smaller groups of ships cruised over limited areas.

PAY UP OR ELSE
19th-century Chinese pirates used to extort money from coastal villages. They threatened to destroy the town and enslave the occupants if the ransom was not paid. In this ransom note, pirates demand money in return for not attacking shipping.

PIRATE PENNANT

The fleets of the China Sea pirates were divided into squadrons, each with their own flags – Ching Yih's fleet had red, yellow, green, blue, black, and white flag groups – and flag carriers led the attack when the pirates boarded a ship. This elaborate flag depicts the mythical empress of heaven T'ien Hou, calmer of storms and protector of merchant ships.

Though the pirates worshiped T'ien Hou, she was also sacred to those who opposed piracy

Bats were a good-luck symbol – their name in Chinese, fu, *is a pun on "good fortune"*

LAST STAND

The British navy destroyed the most notorious Chinese pirate fleet in 1849. Anchored at the mouth of the Haiphong River in northern Vietnam, Shap'n'gtzai thought he was safe. But when the tide turned, it swung the pirate junks around so that their guns pointed at each other. The British ships were able to pick them off one by one.

Naval surgeon Edward Cree captured the destruction of Shap'n'gtzai's fleet in a vivid watercolor painting in his journal

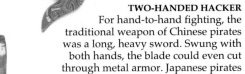

TWO-HANDED HACKER

For hand-to-hand fighting, the traditional weapon of Chinese pirates was a long, heavy sword. Swung with both hands, the blade could even cut through metal armor. Japanese pirates preferred smaller swords: they fought with one in each hand and could defeat even the most skilled Chinese warrior.

Punishment

"DANCING THE HEMPEN JIG" was the punishment for pirates caught and convicted of their crimes. The "hempen jig" was the dance of death at the end of the hangman's hemp rope. Pirates joked about execution, but this bravado often vanished when they were faced with the gallows. However, for most pirates, the everyday dangers of life at sea were more of a hazard than the hangman. Relatively few were brought to justice, and even those found guilty were often pardoned. For privateers, capture meant only imprisonment, with the possibility of freedom through an exchange of prisoners. But many privateers feared prison; jails were disease-ridden places from which many never returned.

Head of a pirate displayed on a pike

Wooden gallows were usually specially built for each execution

Hempen rope

THE HANGMAN'S NOOSE
Hanging was a traditional punishment for pirates. When executed in England or one of its colonies, pirates were hanged at the low-tide mark to show that their crimes came under the jurisdiction of the Admiralty. Pirates' last words were often recorded and published for the delight of the public.

PRISON HULKS
Britain introduced these floating prisons in 1776. Moored in the estuary of the river Thames, hulks were first made from naval ships that were no longer seaworthy. Later hulks were specially built as floating jails. Conditions inside a prison hulk were damp and unhealthy, and being consigned to one was the severest punishment apart from the death sentence.

THE PRISONER PAYS
A solitary cell like this one would have been considered luxury accommodations by a captive pirate. Prison cells in the 17th and 18th centuries were crowded to the bursting point, and only those who could afford to bribe the jailer could hope to live in decent conditions. Prisoners paid for candles, food, and even for the right to get close to the feeble fire that warmed the dank dungeon.

THE PONTON
Captured French corsairs dreaded English prison hulks, which they called *pontons*. One wrote in 1797, "For the last eight days we have been reduced to eating dogs, cats and rats…the only rations we get consist of mouldy bread… rotten meat, and brackish water."

Extension to ship may have been the prison ship's galley

Laundry hung out to dry

Prisoners lived in the damp, stinking hold

Ventilation through tiny windows was poor

Soldier guards the prison hulk

THE END OF THE LINE

Like many a pirate's hanging, that of Stede Bonnet in 1718 was a public event. The people of Charleston, South Carolina, crowded the docks to get a view. The once dashing Major Bonnet had begged the Governor for a reprieve, but his pleas were in vain.

Skull of an 18th-century murderer

HANGING IN CHAINS

The bodies of executed pirates were often hung from a wooden frame called a gibbet to warn others not to repeat their crimes. The corpse was chained into an iron cage to prevent relatives from taking it down and burying it. A condemned man was measured for his gibbet chains before his execution, and pirates were said to fear this even more than hanging.

Tight-fitting cage ensured that the bones stayed in place once the flesh had rotted

Broad iron band enclosed the arms and chest

Gibbet cage was made to measure by a blacksmith

Handcuffs

NO ESCAPE

Pirates were often put in chains to prevent attempts at escape. Before being shipped to England, the unfortunate William Kidd spent the winter of 1699 secured in a Boston jail by manacles weighing more than 16 lb (7 kg).

Early 19th-century ankle fetters

18th-century gibbet cage

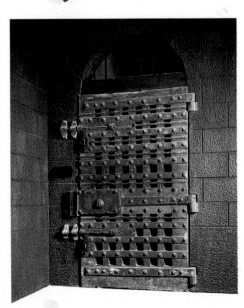

ABANDON HOPE, ALL YE WHO ENTER

William Kidd and other pirates walked through this grim gate into London's infamous Newgate Prison. Kidd was held in this foul, overcrowded jail for an entire year. By the time of his trial, he was in no fit state to defend himself.

A GRIM REMINDER

The hanging of William Kidd (p. 46) in 1701 drew a large crowd to London's Execution Dock. After the first rope snapped, Kidd was hanged in the second attempt. His corpse was chained to a post to be washed three times by the tide, according to Admiralty law. Kidd's body was then covered in tar to make it last and hung in chains at Tilbury Point, where it served as a warning to all seamen sailing in or out of the Thames River.

The pirates defeated

AFTER FLOURISHING for 5,000 years, organized piracy and privateering finally ended in the 19th century. At the turn of the century, privateers were still a dangerous nuisance – yet the navies of big maritime powers no longer needed the help of privately owned warships. So in 1856, most nations signed a treaty, the Declaration of Paris, banning letters of marque. Technology also helped to end piracy. The 19th century was the age of steam power, and the navies of Britain and the U.S. built steamships that could sail anywhere, even on a windless day. Pirates in their sailing ships relied on the wind and were easily trapped by the steamers. By 1850, only a few small bands of pirates were left.

JUSTICE – OR REVENGE?
The British Royal Navy took strong action against Malaysian and Indonesian pirates suspected of damaging trade. This colorful figurehead once decorated the bow of HMS *Harlequin*, a naval sloop that sailed from Penang, Malaysia, in 1844 aiming to punish pirates from north Sumatra. The *Harlequin* and another sloop and steamer could not identify the pirates they were seeking, so the little fleet indiscriminately burned down riverside houses.

HEAD OF A PIRATE
Blackbeard's head was suspended from the end of the bowsprit of the *Pearl*.

LAST-DITCH BATTLE
As in life, Blackbeard was a legend in death: "He fought with great fury until he received five-and-twenty wounds, and five of them by shot." Lieutenant Maynard, of the Royal Navy sloop *Pearl*, which captured the pirate, had Blackbeard's head cut off and hung from the end of the bowsprit (the spar at the front of the ship).

STEAMING AGAINST THE PIRATES
The first steamships had masts and sails, but they could also be propelled by paddle wheels. Pirates ignored the smoking vessels when they first saw them, assuming they were sailing ships on fire. Their nonchalance ended when the steamers sailed directly against the wind (impossible in a sailing ship) to capture them.

POLICE DOG
When HMS *Greyhound* sighted two ships to the east of Long Island, the crew could not have known just what dangerous pirates they were tangling with. After an eight-hour battle, the *Greyhound* brought Edward Low (p. 30) and his crew to justice. In the summer of 1723, 26 of the pirates were hanged.

THE *SWALLOW*
The Royal Navy's ultimate "pirate buster" was a man-of-war, a huge sailing fortress that could outgun the most powerful pirate ship. The man-of-war *Swallow* brought an end to the career of notorious pirate Bartholomew Roberts (p. 31) off the West African coast in 1722. Roberts foolishly sailed into a battle against the warship and was shot in the neck.

BOMBING BARBARY
Corsairs sailing from the Barbary states (pp. 14–15) renewed their attacks during the Napoleonic Wars (1796–1815). When peace returned, the U. S. and the European powers acted to crush the Barbary pirates for good. In 1816, British and Dutch ships bombarded the Algerian port of Algiers, forcing the Bey (p. 14) to release prisoners and apologize for the pirates' actions. France occupied Algiers 14 years later.

CELEBRATING VICTORY
Inscribed "Algiers bombarded and its fleet destroyed and Christian slavery extinguished," this gold medal celebrates the successful British and Dutch bombardment of Algiers.

View of the *Swallow*'s bows

Due to naval cutbacks, figurehead has less elaborate carving than on earlier ships

Imprisoned pirates from Roberts's ship were held in manacles in the hold

Roberts was killed by grapeshot from one of these guns

With 50 cannon and a highly trained crew, the Swallow *easily outgunned Roberts's* Royal Fortune *and its ragged pirate band*

Side view of the *Swallow*

Pirates in literature

Almost as soon as the world's navies had made the oceans safe, people began to forget the pirates' murderous ways. Many writers turned pirates from thieves into rascals or heroes. But books do not always paint a romantic picture of piracy. Some, such as *Buccaneers of America*, tell true pirate stories in blood-curdling detail. And in the most famous of all fictional tales, *Treasure Island*, the pirates are villains to be feared. Yet even this classic adventure yarn revolves around the search for a buried hoard of gold. Like walking the plank, buried treasure is exciting and colorful – but fiction nonetheless.

BAD BIRD
"Pieces of eight!" Long John Silver's parrot called out for the fictional pirate's favorite booty.

BYRONIC HERO
English poet Lord Byron (1788–1824) did much to create the myth of the romantic pirate. He wrote his famous poem *The Corsair* at a time when the pirate menace was only a few years in the past. Byron excuses the crimes of his hero with the rhyme "He knew himself a villain but he deem'd The rest no better than the thing he seem'd."

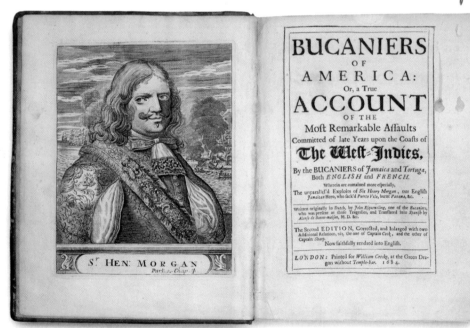

Sr HEN: MORGAN
Part. 2. Chap. 4.

BUCANIERS
OF
AMERICA:
Or, a True
ACCOUNT
OF THE
Moſt Remarkable Aſſaults
Committed of late Years upon the Coaſts of
The Weſt-Indies.
By the BUCANIERS of *Jamaica* and *Tortuga*,
Both *ENGLISH* and *FRENCH*.
Wherein are contained more eſpecially,
The unparallel'd Exploits of Sir Henry Morgan, our Engliſh Jamaican Hero, who ſack'd *Puerto Velo*, burnt *Panama*, &c.
Written originally in Dutch, by *John Eſquemeling*, one of the *Bucaniers*, who was preſent at thoſe Tragedies, and Tranſlated into Spaniſh by *Alonſo de Bonne-maiſo*, M. D. &c.
The Second EDITION, Corrected, and Inlarged with two Additional Relations, viz. the one of Captain *Cook*, and the other of Captain *Sharp*.
Now faithfully rendered into Engliſh.
LONDON: Printed for *William Crooke*, at the Green Dragon without Temple-bar. 1684.

TRUE STORIES OF PIRATE VILLAINY
Alexander Exquemeling (1645–1707) provided one of the few eyewitness accounts of 17th-century piracy. A Frenchman, he sailed with buccaneers in the Caribbean. His vivid descriptions of their cruelty, first published in Dutch in 1678, are still capable of making the reader feel physically sick.

IN SEARCH OF TREASURE
In *Treasure Island*, Jim Hawkins, who narrates the story, sets sail in the *Hispaniola* to unearth a pirate's buried booty. Jim overhears a plan by Silver and Israel Hands to capture the ship and kill the crew.

PIRATE WITH PARROT
When Scottish writer Robert Louis Stevenson (1850–94) created Long John Silver, he invented a pirate who has influenced writers ever since. Silver quickly gains the treasure-seekers' trust in *Treasure Island* (1883), only to betray them later.

MYTHICAL MAP
The key to the treasure in Stevenson's book is an island map and cryptic clues. No real pirate left such convenient directions to a fortune.

WALKING TO A WATERY GRAVE

Boston stationer Charles Ellms published *The Pirates' Own Book* in 1837. A mixture of myth and "true" pirate stories, it quickly became a bestseller. Ellms described the pirate punishment of "walking the plank," but there is only one documented case of this occurring, when pirates forced Dutch sailors from the captured *Vhan Fredericka* to walk to their deaths in 1829.

IN A TIGHT CORNER

"One more step, Mr. Hands … and I'll blow your brains out." Mutinous buccaneer Israel Hands ignored Jim Hawkins's warning, only to be sent plunging to his death by a blast from the boy's flintlock. Robert Louis Stevenson borrowed the name for this fictional villain from Blackbeard's real-life first mate.

MYSTERY HISTORY

A General History of the Robberies and Murders of the Most Notorious Pyrates was published in 1724. It describes the exploits of pirates such as Blackbeard, Bartholomew Roberts, Mary Read, and Anne Bonny within a few years of their capture or execution. The book inspired many later works of fiction, but the true identity of its author, Captain Charles Johnson, is a mystery.

St JOHN FALSTAFF and his Companions at GAD'S HILL.

A General
HISTORY
OF THE
LIVES and ADVENTURES
Of the Most Famous

Highwaymen, Murderers, Street-Robbers, &c

From the Famous

Sir *John Falstaff* in the Reign of K. *Henry* IV, 1399 to 1733.

To which is added,

A Genuine Account of the *VOYAGES* and *PLUNDERS* of the most Notorious *PYRATES*.

Interfperfed with diverting TALES, and pleafant SONGS.

And Adorned with Six and Twenty Large Copper Plates, Engraved by the beft Mafters.

By Capt. CHARLES JOHNSON.

— *Little Villains oft' fubmit to Fate,
That Great Ones may enjoy the World in State.*

GARTH.

LONDON;
Printed for and Sold by OLIVE PAYNE, at Horace's-Head, in Round-Court in the Strand, over-againft York-Buildings.
M.DCC.XXXVI.

PIRATES ON THE PAGE

Thousands of children saw the play *Peter Pan*. But the book, first published as *Peter and Wendy*, charmed millions more. Set on a magic island and a pirate ship, the story tells of the defeat of pirates by a boy who never grew up.

PAN AND HOOK

Peter Pan's adversary, Captain Hook, was in fiction "Blackbeard's bosun," and author J. M. Barrie (1860–1937) took some of Hook's character from the real pirate Edward Teach (pp. 30–31). "His hair was dressed in long curls which at a little distance looked like black candles."

Peter and Hook fought for their lives on a slippery rock, but only Peter fought fairly

Pirates in film and theater

SWAGGERING ON THE SCREEN or swooping across the stage, a pirate provided dramatists with a ready-made yet adaptable character. He could play a black-hearted villain, a carefree adventurer, a romantic hero, or a blameless outlaw. Theatrical pirates first trod the boards in 1612, but it was *The Successful Pirate* a century later that really established the theme. Moviemakers were also quick to exploit the swashbuckling glamour of the pirate life. Screen portrayals of piracy began in the era of the silent films and they remain a box-office draw to this day.

THESPIAN PIRATE
This 19th-century souvenir shows an actor named Pitt playing the pirate Will Watch, with the standard pirate props.

STAGE SUIT
Neatly pressed stage costumes contrast vividly with the rags that real pirates wore. Most real pirates changed their clothes only when they raided a ship and stole a new set.

Puppet's head is made of wood

Curved cutlass

PUPPET PARODY
The action and speed of buccaneering stories makes them a natural choice for puppet theaters. In a crude satire of pirate style, these two 19th-century glove puppets depict English and Spanish pirates. The simply dressed English pirate carries the short, curved cutlass; his dapper Spanish counterpart holds a rapier.

English pirate puppet

NEVERLAND COMES TO TINSELTOWN
In Steven Spielberg's remake of the Peter Pan story *Hook*, Dustin Hoffman played the title role.

CORSAIR CRAZY
In the early 1950s pirate movies were very popular—nine films appeared between 1950 and 1953. The *Crimson Pirate*, starring Burt Lancaster (1952) was one of the best.

HIRSUTE HEADGEAR
When an explosion blew him from his ship, one of Bartholomew Roberts' (p. 31) crew ignored his injuries and complained that he had "lost a good hat by it." It was probably not as grand as this costume hat.

SWASHBUCKLER'S SCARF
Early pirate movies may have favored red and yellow props such as this sash because they showed up better than other colors on the primitive Technicolor film system. Burning ships were popular for the same reason.

Spanish pirate puppet

Rapier

SHOW DOWN
Hollywood told the true story of pirate Anne Bonny (p. 33) in *Anne of the Indies* (1951), but the temptation to dress up history was, as usual, too much to resist. The movie pitted Anne, played by American actress Jean Peters (born 1926) against her "former boss" Blackbeard—even though the two never actually met or sailed together.

STICK UP
Captain Blood was based on a book by Italian-born British writer Rafael Sabatini (1875–1950). This poster for the French version illustrates how the film industry transformed the pirate into a romantic hero.

CARIBBEAN PIRATES
Pirates of the Caribbean: The Curse of the Black Pearl (2003) starred Johnny Depp as Jack Sparrow. This rip-roaring blockbuster and its sequels (Jack Sparrow fights again in *Dead Man's Chest*, right) are proof of Hollywood's continuing fascination with the excitement and glamour of pirate life.

Did you know?

FASCINATING FACTS

Bartholemew Roberts's success may have been due to the fact he was not a typical pirate. He was smart, only drank tea, never swore, and observed the Sabbath!

In the 17th century, the East India Company was so plagued by pirates that the British Admiralty granted the company permission to catch and punish pirates itself. Punishments included hanging at the yardarm, taking the prisoner to be flogged by every ship at anchor, and branding a man's forehead with the letter P.

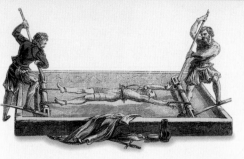

Jean Bart teaches his son a lesson

During a battle with a Dutch ship, French corsair Jean Bart noticed his 14-year-old son flinching at the sound of gunfire. Displeased by this cowardice, Bart had his son tied to the mast, saying to his crew, "It is necessary that he should get accustomed to this sort of music."

Good maps and sea charts were rare and highly prized because they were the key to power and wealth in new territories. When Bartholemew Sharp captured a Spanish ship in 1681, the crew tried to throw the book of sea charts overboard rather than hand it over. Sharp got hold of the book just in time, and it is said that the Spanish cried when they saw him take it.

Rats have always been a serious problem on board ship for all sailors—including pirates—and they were often hunted to keep numbers down. One Spanish galleon reported killing more than 4,000 rats on a voyage from the Caribbean to Europe.

The buccaneers would do anything for money—they were known to stretch their victims on racks to get them to tell where they had hidden their treasures.

A ship's log book got its name from the "log," a plank tied to a rope and hurled overboard to measure a ship's speed.

Boarding a ship was very dangerous and, if already under fire, the first pirate on board faced almost certain death. To encourage men to join boarding parties, the rule on many ships was that the first to board got first choice of any weapon plundered on top of his share of the haul. The chance to own a highly prestigious weapon like a pistol was usually enough to persuade someone to chance his luck.

A boarding party

To careen means to turn a ship on its side. Pirates did this because, unlike other sailors, they could not go into dry dock for repairs and removal of the barnacles that affected a ship's speed and mobility. So a ship was run aground in a shallow bay, unloaded, and pulled onto its side for cleaning. It was then turned over so the other side could be done.

Blackbeard's fate

Relatively few pirates were hanged for their crimes or met colorful, gruesome ends. Blackbeard suffered 22 blows before his head was chopped off and hung from the bowsprit as a warning. Most died from fighting, drowning, and disease. On a long voyage, it was not uncommon for a captain to lose half his crew to diseases such as typhoid, malaria, scurvy, and dysentery.

Pirate ships rarely attacked a man-of-war because of its superior firepower, so a warship escorting a treasure ship would often set a trap. It would keep its distance, waiting on the horizon until a pirate ship approached the treasure ship, then move in swiftly for the attack.

Blackbeard once fell in love with a pretty girl who turned him down for another seaman. The girl gave the man a ring as a token of her love. As the story goes, Blackbeard later attacked the sailor's ship and, seeing the ring, cut off the man's hand and sent it to the girl in a silver box. At the sight of the hand and the ring, the poor girl fainted and later died of grief.

Pirate Henry Morgan loved to drink

Q Do pirates really deserve their reputation as drunkards?

A It is not surprising that pirates had a reputation for drunkenness—their ration of alcohol was greater than that for water. Supplies of water on board ship were limited and quickly went bad, so sailors preferred to drink bottled beer, rum, or grog (water mixed with rum to disguise the taste and help preserve it). The buccaneers are even said to have drunk a mixture of rum and gunpowder!

Q Are there still pirates active in the oceans of the world today?

A Yes, piracy is still a problem today. The area worst affected is the South China Seas, but the waters off East Africa are dangerous, too. Merchant ships and luxury yachts are the most common targets, but in 1992 pirates attacked an oil tanker. It has become such a problem that, in 1992, a Piracy Reporting Center was set up in Kuala Lumpur, Malaysia.

Q In pictures, pirates are often shown wearing earrings—is this right?

A Probably not. Earrings for men were not fashionable during the golden age of piracy. They began appearing in pictures of pirates in the 1890s.

Q Did pirates really like to keep parrots as pets?

A There are no accounts of any well-known pirates having parrots as pets. But there was a trade in exotic animals throughout the age of piracy. A colorful talking bird would have been worth quite a bit of money, and as pirates stole anything of value, they probably took some parrots, too. The crew would surely have been glad to have these intelligent birds around to provide a bit of entertainment on long, dull voyages.

Q Were there pirates with wooden legs, like Long John Silver in the book *Treasure Island*?

A Yes, the successful 16th-century French privateer Francois le Clerc was known as "Pied de Bois" because he had a wooden leg. However, peg-leg pirates were rare. Sailing a ship is a job for the able-bodied. If a sailor of any sort lost a limb, it usually meant the end of his career at sea. One exception was the cook—a job traditionally reserved for anyone who was disabled.

Q Was a marlinspike a tool or a weapon?

A A marlinspike was an essential tool for unraveling ropes. But to a mutinous crew, its sharp point made it a potential weapon. This was because, to keep control of his ship, a captain locked up all weapons until just before an attack. So a marlinspike might be the only likely object the crew could lay their hands on.

Q Surely a pirate stood a good chance of surviving being marooned?

A Marooning was a terrible punishment because it meant a slow death. Pirates were usually marooned on islands where they stood little chance of surviving—a rocky outcrop, a sandspit that was covered by the tide, or a place with little vegetation. Even if a ship did spot a man, knowing of this pirate punishment, the crew was unlikely to pick him up. The pistol given to a marooned man was most often used by the pirate to end his own misery.

Q Did pirates ever steal possessions from one another?

A They almost certainly tried to, but there were strict rules to stop this from happening. A pirate code states that any pirate caught stealing from another should have his ears and nose slit and then be put ashore somewhere he was sure to encounter hardship.

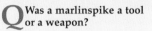

Record Breakers

☠ **CRUELEST PIRATE**
There are many contenders for this title, among them French buccaneer Francis L'Ollonais and English pirate Edward Low.

☠ **MOST SUCCESSFUL PIRATE**
Welshman Bartholomew Roberts captured around 400 ships in his lifetime.

☠ **MOST USELESS PIRATE**
Pirate Edward England was marooned by his crew for showing too much mercy toward his prisoners.

☠ **RICHEST PIRATE HAUL**
This was possibly Henry Avery's capture of the *Gang-i-Sawai* with a haul of $500,000. Each man got more than $3,000—the equivalent of which would be millions today.

☠ **MOST FEARSOME PIRATE**
Edward Teach, known as Blackbeard, terrified everybody—even his own crew—yet it is not clear that he killed anyone until the battle in which he died. He operated for just two years yet established a terrifying reputation.

Ships vanish as piracy rules

John Sweeney reports on the brutal buccaneers plundering cargo lanes

A newspaper report on modern piracy

Edward England

Who's who?

It's impossible to list here all the pirates, privateers, corsairs, and buccaneers who once sailed the oceans of the world, but below are profiles of some of the most notorious characters in this book, who were active in the golden age of piracy, between the 16th and 19th centuries.

HENRY AVERY
1665–c. 1728
English pirate Henry Avery was legendary for his brutal capture of the valuable Arab ships the *Faleh Mohammed* and the *Gang-i-Sawai* in the Red Sea, in 1695. He was never caught but died a pauper, not leaving enough to buy a coffin.

BARBAROSSA BROTHERS
ACTIVE 1500–1546
Barbary corsairs Kheir-ed-din and Aruj Barbarossa were feared for their attacks on Christian settlements and ships in the Mediterranean. Aruj was killed in battle, but Kheir-ed-din went on to establish the Barbary States as a Mediterranean power.

JEAN BART
1651–1702
Frenchman Jean Bart was the leader of a band of privateers operating in the English Channel and North Sea. In 1694, Bart was honored by King Louis XIV of France for his achievements.

ANNE BONNY
ACTIVE 1720
American Anne Bonny fell into piracy when she ran off with pirate captain Jack Rackham. Disguised as a man, she helped him plunder ships in the Caribbean, but they were captured, and Rackham went to the gallows. Bonny escaped the death penalty because she was pregnant.

CHING SHIH
1807–1810
Madame Ching Shih was the widow of a Chinese pirate captain but turned out to be an even greater pirate leader than her husband. With 1,800 armed junks and around 80,000 men and women, she had total control over the coastal trade around China.

Anne Bonny

CHUI APOO
DIED 1851
Chui Apoo led a pirate stronghold of around 600 vessels off the coast of Hong Kong. In 1849 he was cornered by a British naval force, and his fleet was destroyed. Apoo escaped, but was betrayed by his followers and captured.

Chui Apoo

HOWELL DAVIS
ACTIVE 1719
Welsh pirate Howell Davis operated off Africa's Guinea Coast. He is most famous for his bold capture of two French ships by forcing the crew of the first ship to act as pirates and fly a black flag. The second ship, believing it was surrounded by pirates, quickly surrendered.

CHARLOTTE DE BERRY
BORN 1636
Charlotte de Berry disguised herself as a man to join the English Navy with her husband. She was later forced onto a ship bound for Africa, and when the captain discovered her secret, he attacked her. De Berry took revenge by leading a mutiny and turning the ship to piracy. She operated off the African coast, raiding ships carrying gold.

SIR FRANCIS DRAKE
C. 1540–1596
Sir Francis Drake was a British privateer and pirate, whose success at plundering Spanish ships in the New World made both himself and the English queen, Elizabeth I, very rich. He was the first Englishman to circumnavigate the globe and was knighted in 1581. He also became a popular naval hero after his defeat of the Spanish Armada in 1588. He died of a fever in Panama.

RÉNÉ DUGUAY-TROUIN
1673–1736
Duguay-Trouin was the son of a St. Malo shipping family and joined the French Navy at age 16. By the age of 21, he commanded a 40-gun ship. He was the most famous of the French corsairs and was so successful he became an admiral in the French Navy.

Réné Duguay-Trouin

EDWARD ENGLAND
ACTIVE 1718–1720
Edward England was an English pirate who sailed for a time with Bartholomew Roberts. He had some success until his crew marooned him with two others on the island of Mauritius for being too humane to a prisoner. It is said that they built a boat and escaped to Madagascar.

John Paul Jones

JOHN PAUL JONES
1747–1792
John Paul Jones was born in Scotland, but he fled to America to escape a murder charge. He joined the American Navy during the American Revolution (1755–83) to fight against the British, and became famous for his daring captures of British ships.

WILLIAM KIDD
C. 1645–1701

William Kidd was an American businessman who was sent to the Indian Ocean to hunt pirates—but he was forced to raid vessels by his mutinous crew. Bad luck continued to follow Kidd, and on his return to America, he was arrested and sent to England to stand trial for piracy. He was found guilty and hanged. His body was displayed in public to warn seamen of the high price pirates paid for their crimes.

JEAN LAFITTE
C. 1780–C. 1826

Jean Lafitte ran privateering and smuggling operations in the Gulf of Mexico from a base on Galveston Island, Texas. Although Lafitte was outlawed for trading in slaves and attacking vessels that were not covered by letters of marque, he was pardoned because of his brave defense of New Orleans against the British in 1812.

Edward Teach, also known as Blackbeard

William Kidd

FRANCIS L'OLLONAIS
ACTIVE C. 1660s

L'Ollonais was a French buccaneer notorious for his cruelty. He is said to have cut open a poor Spaniard with his cutlass, pulled out his victim's heart, and gnawed on it, threatening the other prisoners that this would be their fate if they didn't talk.

EDWARD LOW
ACTIVE 1720s

English pirate Edward Low was famous for his cruelty to both prisoners and his crew. His violence drove his men to mutiny, and they set him adrift in a rowboat with no provisions. Incredibly, Low was rescued by another ship the following day.

HENRY MORGAN
C. 1635–1688

Welshman Henry Morgan was a buccaneer and privateer operating out of Port Royal in Jamaica. He was a great leader and became legendary for his brilliant and brutal raids on Spanish colonies, for which he was knighted.

JACK RACKHAM
ACTIVE 1718–1720

The English pirate captain Jack Rackham was also known as "Calico Jack" because he liked to wear colorful calico cotton clothes. He operated in the Caribbean but is perhaps best-known as the husband of pirate Anne Bonny. He was hanged for piracy in Port Royal, Jamaica.

MARY READ
1690–1720

Mary Read dressed as a man from childhood to claim an inheritance and went on to serve in both the army and navy. She joined the crew of pirate Jack Rackham, where she met fellow female pirate Anne Bonny. The two women were said to have fought more bravely than any of the men. Like Bonny, she escaped hanging because she was pregnant, but she died of an illness soon after.

BARTHOLOMEW ROBERTS
1682–1722

Dashing Welshman Bartholomew Roberts was forced into piracy when his ship was seized by pirates, yet he went on to become one of the most successful pirates ever. He operated in the Caribbean and off the Guinea coast. He was killed in a battle with an English man-of-war.

BARTHOLOMEW SHARP
C. 1650–1690

In 1680–82, English buccaneer Bartholomew Sharp made an incredible expedition along the west coast of South America, around Cape Horn to the West Indies, plundering Spanish colonies. He was let off charges of piracy in exchange for a valuable book of charts that he had stolen from the Spanish.

ROBERT SURCOUF
1773–1827

From his base on the island of Mauritius in the Indian Ocean, French corsair Robert Surcouf plagued British merchant ships trading with India.

EDWARD TEACH (BLACKBEARD)
ACTIVE 1716–1718

Better known as Blackbeard, Edward Teach operated in the Caribbean, terrifying everyone, even his crew, with his wild appearance and violent ways. Finally, he was hunted down by the British Navy and killed, fighting furiously to the very end.

Bartholomew Roberts and two of his ships

Find out more

PIRACY IS A POPULAR subject, and anywhere in the world where pirates were active you will find information about them in local museums. Some of the most exciting new information on this subject has come from salvage work on the wrecks of two pirate ships, the *Whydah* and the *Queen Anne's Revenge*. Information about the wrecks is given below, but the most up-to-date details can be found on the projects' Web sites. Books, however, are still one of the best ways to learn more about pirates. Good sources include original texts written by people who lived with pirates and also modern research.

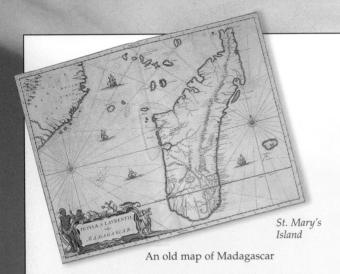
St. Mary's Island

An old map of Madagascar

THE WRECK OF THE *ADVENTURE GALLEY*
In 1698, on St. Mary's Island off Madagascar, William Kidd heard that he was wanted for piracy, set fire to his ship, the *Adventure Galley*, and fled. Barry Clifford (below) found what he believed to be the *Adventure Galley* in 2000. You can read about his search in his book, *Return to Treasure Island and the Search for Captain Kidd*.

THE TREASURE OF THE *WHYDAH*
Diver Barry Clifford is seen here with some treasure from the pirate ship *Whydah*. In 1717, the *Whydah* was wrecked in a storm off New England, killing her captain and 143 of the crew. One of the two survivors told how the ship carried 180 bags of gold and silver plundered from more than 50 ships. Clifford found the wreck in 1984, after a search of 15 years.

THE EXPEDITION *WHYDAH* SEA LAB AND LEARNING CENTER
More than 100,000 artifacts from the *Whydah* have been found, and many are exhibited in the Expedition *Whydah* Center in Provincetown, Massachusetts. Displays in the museum also tell the story of the discovery of the wreck. The *Whydah* is still being salvaged, and, in the summer months, visitors can see new treasures being brought in from the wreck and watch artifacts being conserved.

Places to visit

NORTH CAROLINA MARITIME MUSEUM, Beaufort, North Carolina
See artifacts from Blackbeard's flagship, *Queen Anne's Revenge*, exhibits about the history of life at sea, and a display of wooden boats.

NEW ENGLAND PIRATE MUSEUM, Salem, Massachusetts
An interactive museum with a guided tour of several pirate hangouts, including a colonial port, a pirate ship, and an 80-foot cave.

PIRATES OF NASSAU MUSEUM, Nassau, Bahamas
A museum designed to clear up myths about pirates with tours of nearby pirate sites.

EXPEDITION *WHYDAH* CENTER, Provincetown, Massachusetts
See artifacts from the wreck of the *Whydah* and watch new items undergoing conservation.

THE WRECK OF *QUEEN ANNE'S REVENGE*
In 1717, Blackbeard acquired a French merchant ship, *La Concorde*. He renamed it *Queen Anne's Revenge* and returned to North Carolina together with pirate Stede Bonnet in the *Adventure*. It seems that Blackbeard then ran the *Revenge* aground, tricked Bonnet, and escaped on the *Adventure* with the treasure. In 1996, a wreck was found at Beaufort Inlet, North Carolina. Items found so far include cannons, anchors, sections of the hull, and the ship's bell, dated 1709. The evidence indicates that the wreck is that of the *Queen Anne's Revenge*, but there is as yet no conclusive proof.

The barnacle-encrusted anchor is about 14 ft (4 m) long.

Yellow lines mark out a grid so the site can be mapped.

UNSOLVED PIRATE MYSTERIES

It is said that Blackbeard was once asked if anyone else knew where his treasure was and that he replied, "Only two people know where the treasure lies, the Devil and myself, and he who lives the longest may claim it all." Pirates very rarely buried their treasure, and the few that did left no information about how to find it. But this has not stopped people from looking. There are still famous treasures unaccounted for, and many tantalizing mysteries. Stirred by such stories, some people have spent many years looking for clues about pirates and what might have become of their treasure.

Kidd watches as his men bury his treasure on Gardiner's Island.

THE TREASURE OF COCOS ISLAND

Cocos Island, off Costa Rica, was the perfect place to hide treasure because it was so hard to find. Not only was the island obscured by rain for nine months of the year, but it was inaccurately mapped and strong winds and currents would drive sailors away from it. Three hoards are said to be hidden there: a 17th-century pirate haul, the booty of pirate Benito Bonito, and a fantastic haul known as the Treasure of Lima. But no fortunes have been made there yet. Even German adventurer August Gissler, who spent 17 years on the island, left with just one doubloon.

WHAT HAPPENED TO JEAN LAFITTE?

In 1821, the authorities determined to shut down the highly profitable operations on Galveston Island, Texas, of privateer and smuggler Jean Lafitte. Lafitte knew the game was up and agreed to dismantle his organization. Naval officers watched as Lafitte set fire to his headquarters, and the next day, his ship was gone. Lafitte was never seen again. Was he killed, as some stories suggest, or did he live on under an alias? What happened to the fortune he was known to have amassed? His friends claimed that he had a mania for burying treasure. Although there have been lots of stories, and even more treasure hunters, nothing has ever been found.

BURIED TREASURE

William Kidd is one of the few pirates known to have buried treasure. In 1699, Kidd called in at an island just off New York and asked Lord Gardiner, who lived there, if he could leave some items in his trust. Gardiner agreed, but soon after Kidd was arrested. Kidd's treasure was recovered by the authorities. It included gold, silver, precious stones, jewels, sugar, and silks. Many believed this was not all of his plunder from the Indian Ocean, but no one has ever discovered what happened to the rest.

ISLES OF SHOALS

After Blackbeard's death, all that was recovered was cotton, indigo, sugar, and cocoa—so what about his treasure? One story is that silver and pieces of eight were buried on Smuttynose, one of the Isles of Shoals, New Hampshire, where Blackbeard spent his last months. In 1820 a man building a wall on the island dug up four bars of silver. Were these Blackbeard's, and are there perhaps more on the island?

USEFUL WEB SITES

➤ The official site of the *Queen Anne's Revenge*:
www.ah.dcr.state.nc.us/qar

➤ Expedition *Whydah*:
www.whydah.com

➤ A high-seas adventure, including games and pirate facts:
www.nationalgeographic.com/pirates

➤ Instructions for making your own pirate tools and treasures:
www.piratemuseum.com/pirate.htm

➤ Pirates!—pirate legends and true stories:
www.piratesinfo.com/

Glossary

BARBARY COAST The North African coast of the Mediterranean, where Islamic corsairs (also known as Barbary corsairs) raided European trading ships

BARQUE The term for a large sailing ship with several masts rigged with fore-and-aft sails (not square-rigged)

BECALMED When a sailing ship cannot move because there is no wind

BOW The pointed front of a ship, also known as the prow

BOWSPRIT A long spar that projects out from the front of a ship

A buccaneer

BUCCANEER A pirate or privateer who attacked Spanish ships and prosperous ports in the West Indies and Central America in the 1600s

CAREEN To beach a ship and pull it onto its side so that the hull can be cleaned and repaired

Cat-o'-nine-tails

CAT–O'–NINE TAILS A whip used for punishing sailors, made by unraveling a piece of rope to make nine separate strands. Knots on the end of the strands made the punishment even more painful.

CAULK To repair leaking gaps between the timbers of a ship by filling them with fiber and sealing them with pitch (tar)

CHAIN SHOT A weapon made up of two metal balls chained together. It was used to destroy a ship's rigging, masts, and sails.

CHART A map of land and sea used by sailors for navigation

COLORS Another term for the flags carried by a ship

CORSAIR The term used to describe pirates or privateers who operated in the Mediterranean. The term is also used to refer to the ships sailed by such pirates.

CROW'S NEST A small platform high up on a mast, used as a lookout position

CUTLASS A short sword with a broad blade, first used by buccaneers; a popular weapon for battles at sea because it did not get caught in the rigging

DOUBLOON A Spanish coin made of gold, worth 16 pieces of eight

EAST INDIAMAN A large English or Dutch merchant vessel used to transport valuable cargoes of porcelain, tea, silks, and spices in trade with Asia

A flintlock pistol

FLINTLOCK PISTOL An early type of pistol. When the trigger is pulled, a piece of flint strikes a metal plate to make a spark, which fires the gunpowder.

FORECASTLE The raised deck at the front of a ship. Often abbreviated to "fo'c'sle." A raised deck at the back of a ship is called an aftercastle.

GALLEON A large sailing ship with three or more masts used between the 1500s and 1700s, both as a warship and for transporting Spanish treasure

GALLEY A large ship powered by oars, which were usually operated by galley slaves. Also the term for a ship's kitchen

GALLOWS The wooden frame used for hanging criminals

GIBBET A wooden frame used for displaying the dead bodies of criminals as a warning to others

GRAPPLING IRON A metal hook that is thrown onto an enemy ship to pull it closer and make boarding it easier

HALYARD Nautical term for a rope used to hoist a sail or a flag

HARDTACK Tough, dry ship's biscuits, which made up the main part of a sailor's diet

HEAVE-TO To come to a halt

Aftercastle

Raised forecastle

Crow's nest

Bowsprit

Bow

Hull

Galleon

Points for digging into the woodwork of an enemy ship

Grappling iron

Jolly Roger

HISPANIOLA The former name of the island that is today made up of Haiti and the Dominican Republic

HULKS Naval ships used as floating jails for keeping prisoners

JANISSARY A professional Muslim soldier. Barbary corsairs used Janissaries to attack Christian ships.

JOLLY ROGER The common term for the pirate flag

JUNK A wooden sailing ship commonly used in the Far East and China

KEEL The bottom or flat underneath part of a ship or boat

KETCH A small, two-masted ship or boat

Rigging

Long bowsprit

Stern

Ketch

MALOUINE The term used to describe a person (or ship) from St. Malo in France

MAN-OF-WAR A large naval warship

MARLINSPIKE A pointed tool used for unraveling rope in order to splice it

MAROON To leave someone to his or her fate on a remote island—a common pirate punishment

MIDDLE PASSAGE The middle stage of a slave ship's journey, when it traveled from Africa to the Caribbean with a cargo of slaves to be exchanged for goods

MUTINY To refuse to obey an officer's orders, or to lead a revolt on board ship

NEW WORLD In the 16th and 17th centuries, a term used to describe the continents of North and South America, called "new" because they were only discovered by Europeans after 1492

PIECES OF EIGHT Silver pesos (Spanish coins) that were worth eight reales (another early Spanish coin)

Silver pieces of eight

RATLINES Crossed ropes on the shrouds (the ropes which run from the side of the ship to the mast) that form a rope ladder enabling sailors to climb to the top of the mast

RIGGING The arrangement of ropes that support a ship's sails and mast

SCHOONER A small, fast sailing ship with two or sometimes three masts. The fore (front) mast is shorter than the mainmast.

SCURVY A disease, with symptoms including bleeding gums and sores, caused by the lack of vitamin C, which is found in fresh fruit and vegetables

SLOOP A small, light single-masted sailing ship

SPANISH MAIN The name for the area of South and Central America once ruled by the Spanish. The term later came to include the islands and waters of the Caribbean.

SPLICE To weave two rope ends together in order to join them

SQUARE-RIGGED Term for a ship carrying square sails set at right angles to the mast

STERN The back end of a ship

WAGGONER A pirate term for a book of sea charts

YARD Nautical term for the wooden pole to which the top of a sail is attached; also known as the yardarm.

A map dating from 1681, showing the coastline around Panama

LATITUDE Position north or south of the equator, measured according to a system of lines drawn on a map parallel with the equator

LETTER OF MARQUE A license or certificate issued by a monarch or a government authorizing the bearer to attack enemy ships

LOG BOOK The book in which details of the ship's voyage are recorded

LONGBOAT The long wooden ships used by Vikings, powered by sail and oars

LONGITUDE Position east or west in the world, measured according to a system of lines drawn on a map from north to south

PIRATE A general term for any person involved in robbery at sea, including buccaneers, corsairs, and privateers

POWDER Common term for gunpowder

PRESS GANG A group of people who rounded up likely men and forced them to join a ship's crew

PRIVATEER A person who is legally entitled by letter of marque to attack enemy ships; also the term used to describe the ships such people used

A waggoner

Index

Acknowledgments

The publisher would like to thank:
The staff of the National Maritime Museum, London, in particular David Spence, Christopher Gray, and Peter Robinson; the staff of the Museum of London, in particular Gavin Morgan and Cheryl Thorogood; the staff of the Musée de Saint-Malo; Judith Fox at Wilberforce House, Hull City Museums and Art Galleries; Caroline Townend at the Museum of the Order of St. John, London; Elizabeth Sandford at Claydon House, Buckinghamshire; David Pawsey, Mayor Beckwith, Councillor Palmer, and Town Clerk Scammell at Rye Town Hall; Admirals Original Flag Loft Ltd., Chatham; Costume consultant Martine Cooper; French consultant Dan Lallier; Classical consultant Dr. Philip de Souza; Brigadier G. H. Cree for his kind permission to let us reproduce illustrations from the Journal of Edward Cree; David Pickering, Helena Spiteri, and Phil Wilkinson for editorial help; Sophy D'Angelo, Ivan Finnegan, Andrew Nash, Kati Poynor, Aude Van Ryn, Sharon Spencer, Susan St. Louis, and Vicky Wharton for design help; Claire Bowers, Sunita Gahir, Joanne Little,

Nigel Ritchie, Susan St Louis, and Bulent Yusef for help with the clip-art; Neville Graham, Rose Horridge, Joanne Little, and Sue Nicholson for help with the wall chart.

Additional photography by Peter Anderson (12al, ar, cl; 13ar, b), Michele Byam (49cl), John Chase (28cl cr; 31br; 32cl; 33bc; 36bl; 37al, cl, bl; 43ar, c, cr, bl, br; 45al, tr, c, br; 48bl; 62al; 63ar), Stephen Dodd (8br; 9cr; 10cl; 11al, cr, br), Charles Howson (9ar; 22cl; 36ar), Colin Keates (46bl; 52cr), Dave King (61ar), Nick Nicholls (8c; 9b; 10br; 11cl), Richard Platt (34al), Peter Robinson (16cl; 17; 20–21c), James Stephenson (62–63c), Michel Zabé (21ac)

Picture credits
a=above, b=below, c=center, l=left, r=right, t=top

Ancient Art and Architecture Collection: 7trb, 9tl, 16tl. **Art Archive:** 21cr, 21br, 22br, 29tl, 39bl. **Bridgeman Art Library, London:** 18cr; /British Museum 18cl; / Christies, London 53trb; / National Portrait Gallery 18cl, 18cr;

/ National Maritime Museum 38c; London / New York: Private Collection 7b, 46; Victoria & Albert Museum, London 6t. © The British Museum: 7t, 9t, 10b, 10t, 12. The Master and Fellows of Corpus Christi College, Cambridge: 12cb. Corbis: 68cr. Delaware Art Museum: 49tl. Mary Evans Picture Library: 6b, 7tr, 8bl, 9b, 12c, 13bra, 15tlb, 18tr, 20, 20tr, 22, 26tr, 27t, 28, 33b, 35tlb, 35c, 36, 36c, 37tr, 39br, 39tl, 43cb, 47cr, 51tc, 54tr, 54trb, 56cl, 60bl. Kevin Fleming Photography: 9tl. John Frost Historical Newspapers: 65bl. Ronald Grant Archive: 6tlb, 62bl, 63c, 63tl, 63cr. Sonia Halliday Photographs: 9trb. Robert Harding Picture Library: 19b. The Kobal Collection/Walt Disney Pictures: 63br. Library of Congress: 26c, 42br. Mansell Collection: 40trb, 40bl. Michael Holford: front cover tl; 44tl. Musée de la Marine, Paris: 19trb, 51b, rb. Museum of London: 27c, 35t, 40, 56cra, 57bl. The National Maritime Museum: 6tl, 14bl; 14cr, 16, 16c, 18b, 18t, 19t, 22bl, 23, 23tl, 24cl, 25br, 25t, 29, 29tl, 29tr, 29cl, 30, 31tr, 32tl, 32bl, 32cl, 33br, 33rc, 33cb, 33t, 42b, 44bla, 44t, 45tc, 45bc, 47, 51tr, 54tr, 54trb, 58trb, 59c, 58br. The National Portrait Gallery, London: 60tl. Peter Newark's Historical Pictures: 15 br, 22cl, 53br. Richard Platt: 34tl. Public Record Office: Crown copyright material 31t.

Range / Bettman: 22tr, 53cr, 52br. Reproduced with the kind permission of The Trustees of the Ulster Museum: 29ca. Rye Town Hall: 34. Treasure World: 38. Courtesy of the Trustees of the Victoria and Albert Museum / J. Stevenson: 63l. Whydah Management Company: 41c, 42cl. World's Edge Picture Library: 22tl, 49cl. Zentralbibliothek Zurich: 13tl.

Jacket credits: Front: Richard T. Nowitz/Corbis, b; National Maritime Museum, London, UK, tcl, tc; Museum of London, UK, tcr. Back: Mary Evans Picture Library: back br, back tr.

Maps: Eugene Fleury (10cr, 14ar, 20cl, 38cl, 46cl, 54cr).

Wall chart picture credits: DK Images: 95th Rifles and Re-enactment Living History Unit 1cra; British Museum 1bc; Musée de Saint-Malo, France 1ca, 1fcra, 1ftr; Museum of the Order of St John, London 1cr; National Maritime Museum, London: 1cb, 1cla, 1fcr, 1tc; 1fclb (Mary Read)

All other images © Dorling Kindersley
For further information see:
www.dkimages.com